The Manager's Pocket Guide to Innovation

Dr. Richard Brynteson

HRD Press ❖ Amherst, MA

ISBN 978-1-59996-197-2

Production services by Jean Miller
Cover design by Eileen Klockars
Editorial services by Suzanne Bay

Dedication

This book is dedicated to Dr. Rev. Robert DeWerff, excellent scholar, compassionate administrator, and wonderful human being.

The Manager's Pocket Guide to Innovation

Table of Contents

Introduction

Innovation is necessary for survival. This statement is true for individuals as well as for organizations. In order for us to be competitive as individuals, as organizations, and indeed, as a nation, we need to constantly add more value for our clients, customers, and constituencies. We do this through innovation.

The innovation journey is fraught with obstacles. Naysayers line the route with catcalls, such as *"We tried that before"* and *"That will never work here."* Organizational potholes and boulders are strewn across the road. False starts and market shifts lead us down the wrong paths. Weariness from steep learning curves slows the process down. The mountaintop is often enshrouded in the clouds of unending details, stops and starts. Distractions that are part of the day-to-day job tend to shift our focus over and over again.

The journey is necessary, but doing a few important things will keep us going. Keeping close to the customer is central in this journey. Creating a culture of openness is also important for ongoing innovation efforts. A mindset of flexibility and inquiry is also helpful for developing and building on ideas. Creative collaboration is essential for moving teams forward toward market introduction.

Each chapter of this book examines one of the important arenas of innovation:

Chapter 1: "Why Innovation" looks at what innovation means and why it is so important.

Chapter 2: "The Innovative Mind" discusses the characteristics and mindsets that facilitate innovative thinking.

Chapter 3: "Building a Culture for Innovation" shows how to create an organizational environment that moves innovation forward.

Chapter 4: "Focus on the Customer" looks at the customer as the center of innovation efforts.

Chapter 5: "The Process of Innovation" examines processes through which ideas become marketable products and services.

Chapter 6: "Creative Collaboration" lays out ideas that will aid groups in making innovation happen.

Chapter 7: "The Future of Innovation" looks ahead at new arenas in innovation.

Chapter 8: "Conclusion" sums up the contents of the book.

Each chapter also contains four additional sections:

"Try This!" Suggests ways to practice innovation.

"Resource." This section highlights a book or video that explores the chapter's central theme.

"Key Points." Five to ten key points from the chapter are summarized in these sections.

"Take the Pulse of Your Organization." Ask yourself these questions in order to evaluate your own or your organization's performance around the central theme of the chapter.

May you improve your own life and the lives of others with the ideas in this book!

Chapter 1:
Why Innovate?

In 1949, Earl Bakken and his brother-in-law started a business repairing medical equipment out of a garage in northeast Minneapolis. At first, they had one hospital as a client; then they added several hospitals. Pretty soon, their work led to clients asking them to modify existing products and design new ones that would improve the quality of life for patients. The two men tinkered and innovated and soon expanded the business to a second garage and then an apartment. Medtronic, a Fortune 500 company, was born.

The Innovation Imperative

Why innovate? Because we have to. Yes, it is a short answer, yet a true answer. *Because we have to.*

Okay. You bought this book, and expect a longer answer. So here's why: Because of what any newspaper says on a given day. Two wars in the Middle East still soak up tax dollars and lives. Global warming is rapidly changing the environment. Schools are failing. Childhood obesity is rampant. More manufacturing employees are being laid off as their jobs are outsourced. Nuclear waste piles up. Asian carp are swimming up the Mississippi River, devouring everything in their path. The Sahara desert is expanding, lowland gorillas are disappearing, and mortgage holders are defaulting. *Enough.*

Is innovation the only answer to our problems? No, but innovation is the key to meeting the biggest challenges facing our world. Is it an easy answer? No, and it will take focus, perseverance, and powerful thinking. But is it worth the effort? Of course it is. We cannot afford *not* to innovate.

> "Innovate or fall behind; the competitive imperative for virtually all businesses today is that simple."
>
> — Dorothy Leonard,
> Harvard Business School

> "CEOs know that ideas and innovations are the most precious currency in the new economy and increasingly the old economy as well."
>
> — Hargadon and Sutton

Do you want 287 more quotes? They are easily attainable. If you want more, Google "innovation" or "reasons for innovation," or go to Wikiquote. But more quotes would make for a fairly boring and useless book, so you will be spared.

Here are some more hidden reasons why you and your organization should start innovating.

7 Good Reasons to Innovate

1. Innovation drives individual wealth in any economy, and provides ways to create new economic growth.

2. An organization's human resources are its best real competitive advantage. Processes, technologies, capital, and products can all be duplicated.

3. Employees who are allowed to innovate and be creative are happier and have higher morale. They use more of their inherent intelligence and feel like they are genuine contributors. As the author-researcher Csikszentmihalyi wrote, "Creativity is so fascinating that when we are involved in it, we feel that we are living more fully than during the rest of life."

4. Do you want happier people? Spark their imaginations and allow them to be curious. Research on positive psychology and happiness suggests that curiosity increases happiness. Curiosity about the world, about products and processes, and about human motivation drive innovation.

5. Are you being asked to do more with less? Who isn't? Solution? You need to be innovative with what you have. Reduce cycle time. Eliminate steps in a process. Reduce energy consumption by 10%. Innovative processes will help you with that.

(continued)

6. The European Union decreed that 2007 was the year of innovation. Do *you* want to fall further behind?

7. There are four kids in an attic in Bangalore, India who want your job and are working until late hours to take it away. They are probably working while you are watching *Grey's Anatomy* on television.

Besides being hard work, *innovation* is fun. The process enlivens and rejuvenates. It breathes new life into individuals and organizations.

World Challenges that Need Solutions

So I have presented many problems—why not solutions? Well, if I had some, I would be wealthy and retired, rather than just a college professor writing books. But let us look at some of these problems through the lens of an innovator.

Sources of Innovation

1. Unexpected Occurrences
2. Incongruities
3. Process Needs
4. Industry and Market Changes
5. Demographic Changes
6. Changes in Perception
7. New Knowledge

Peter Drucker, *Harvard Business School Journal*, 1985, "The Discipline of Innovation"

Global warming. The effort to combat global warming is going to spawn a wide range of new industries. In fact, I bet there will be a Marshall Plan developed to reverse global warming. Grants, energy conservation investment funds, and market initiatives will flood the western world. There will be a flood of children's books about the subject, energy-saving gadgets, better clothes lines (dryers consume way too much energy), warmer sweaters, more-efficient modes of transportation, seminars, clubs, self-warming food, and many other products, services, and initiatives.

Obesity. Type II diabetes is on the rise, threatening to bankrupt our entire health care system for years to come. We will be inundated with new foods, new lifestyles, new diets, new exercise programs, new pills, new classes, new seminars, and new clubs.

9

Being Americans, we will look for easy solutions—silver bullets to solve this problem quickly and efficiently, with no sacrifices on our part.

Addictions. Our addictions are killing us: alcohol, drugs, video games, Ben and Jerry's. Most treatment programs are terribly expensive and very inefficient. Recidivism rates suggest that many of them are ineffective. Are there new processes or systems that will help bring this problem under control?

Shifts in resources. Oil is running low, and there are fewer large discoveries. Currently, copper is in short supply in the United States, driving thieves to rip copper tubing out of abandoned houses and homes under construction. Drinkable water has become a scarce commodity in many parts of the world, as has clean air. Innovative thinking is necessary in order to find substitutes for our shrinking natural resources.

Environmental pollution. The World Health Organization reports that 16 of the most 20 polluted cities in the world are in China. Eastern Europe, after the fall of the Soviet Union, was declared an environmental cesspool. Closer to home, all the manufacturing plants along the Rio Grande in Mexico are creating an environmental nightmare; not coincidentally cancer rates and other diseases are rising among the local population. What innovative air and water purification systems or pollution-abatement systems and processes will save us from the deadly consequences of this?

Eureka Recycling

Eureka Recycling picks up and recycles material in St. Paul and Minneapolis, Minnesota. Their large trucks rumble down the streets every day. In 2007, they commissioned a strategic planner to create a new 25-year strategic plan. Their new plan would not include trucks. Their mission was to remove recyclables from the waste stream such that recycling was not necessary in 25 years. That is an innovative approach! Their model is Aspen, Colorado, whose 25-year plan does not include skiing. Aspen is looking at the eventuality that global warming might claim ample snow as a victim. Thus, this popular skiing center has to create new activities to draw tourists.

Advances in technology. Each advance in technology, whether it be for the iPod, Internet, cell phone, or something else, opens up markets for a variety of other peripheral innovations. For instance, the ringtone industry, nonexistent a decade ago, is now a billion-dollar business! The Internet has spawned a plethora of online businesses. Any new hardware creates a market for new software applications.

11

Demographic shifts. The millennial generation thinks, acts, and consumes differently than do members of Generation X or the Baby Boomers. What new products or services do they want or need? Due to improved health care in developing countries, this newest generation is coming into the world with higher material expectations. The industrialization of India and China has created large new middle classes with higher standards of living. Meanwhile, as the Baby Boomers live extended life spans, they will need new kinds of health care services.

Failing educational systems. Should learning be such a difficult, inefficient, and laborious process? Why do so many children fall through the cracks? Yet learning works in certain places. What processes and systems can work for children of different learning styles, backgrounds, and abilities? What products, services, and processes can speed the learning process, while also enriching it and making it more fun?

Your life. Why shouldn't your life be more innovative? You could be healthier, wealthier, and wiser if you started thinking more creatively. We all need to find new ways to improve living conditions and our own lives.

We must innovate! We must encourage outside-the-box thinking and incorporate innovation into our organizational practices. We must maintain an innovative edge to stay competitive as individuals, as organizations, as a country. We must begin to let go of the status quo and think more creatively if we want to solve the myriad of societal problems that we face.

Try This!

Low-Tech Innovations

Name three major innovations from the past 20 years. If you are like 90% of the people I ask this question, you thought of the Internet, cell phones, Blackberries, GPS positioning, iPods, and other high-tech innovations. Let me suggest three low-tech innovations or innovative ideas:

- *Starbucks*. Starbucks has created a third space that is neither home nor work. It is not about the coffee. It is a sanctuary, a refuge away from the world. Meanwhile, other companies still ask: "Do they drink their coffee at home, or at work?"

- *Harry Potter*. If you or I went to a major publisher and said that we had a 742-page book written for 12-year-old boys, the publisher would laugh us out of the building. But J.K. Rowling carved out a new market space in a struggling industry. Millions of boys and girls

(continued)

13

quit swimming, quit playing video games, and quit playing baseball to dive fully into this seven-book series. These kids (whom experts say cannot focus) clearly focused on these books.

- *Bagged lettuce*. When I was growing up, there was only leaf lettuce or head lettuce. But now... chop, chop, chop. Throw in some croutons and a packet of Caesar dressing, and for three dollars (same as a small mocha), you can have a ready-made salad. And millions are sold.

- Now answer this question: What low-tech innovation has impacted you favorably?

Here's my point: By assuming that innovations have to be high-tech, you are letting yourself off the hook. After all, few of us will invent a Blackberry or an iPod. But we can *still* come up with original ideas.

What is "Innovation"?

"Innovation is the practical application of creative ideas."

That is a good one-line definition for innovation. Here are some other ways of defining it:

- An innovator is a detective searching for a solution to a real problem, a perceived problem, or an invisible problem.

- An innovation has the potential to make the world a better place.

- "To be effective, an innovation has to be simple, and it has to be focused. It should only do one thing; otherwise it confuses people." (Peter Drucker).

- "Today, innovation concerns much more than new product development. It is about reinventing business processes and building entirely new markets that meet untapped customer needs. Most important, as the Internet and globalization widen the pool of new ideas, it's about selecting and executing the right ideas and bringing them to market in record time." (Business Week, April 24, 2006)

- Innovation is more than simply creating a new product. Business processes can be reinvented, and new markets can be created. It's all about coming up with new ideas and executing the best ones.

- An innovation can be a product (e.g., iPod; double mocha skim latte), a service (e.g., text messaging; e-mail addiction treatment), or a process (e.g., new process for putting a product on the market in six months, rather than in two years).

15

- Breakthrough ideas or products come from individuals, organizational teams, and teams comprised of people from different organizations.

- Innovations are not always created from scratch. They can be slight improvements made to existing products (cars with cup holders), services (a coffee shop with a fireplace), or breakthrough products or services that change the nature of an industry (Cirque de Soleil, wireless technology).

- One innovation might take decades to commercialize (hydrogen cells), while another might be created in days (viral marketing of a candidate over the Internet).

- Some innovations save lives (e.g., new kind of heart stent) and others can take lives (more precise hand-held grenade launcher).

A "radical innovation" is an innovation that is life changing or society changing. It might have the power to dramatically reset customer expectations and behaviors, or be able to change the basis for competitive advantage or the industry dynamics.

Art Fry, inventor of Post-it™ Notes, does not believe that a good idea is automatically an innovation; "An idea doesn't become an innovation until it is widely adopted and incorporated into people's daily lives."

Myth vs. Reality

1. **Myth:** Innovation is the domain of solitary creative genius-types.
   Reality: Innovation is the domain of all of us. If we wait for some lone genius to come up with an "aha" moment, we might go out of business.

2. **Myth:** An innovation is always high-tech.
   Reality: Innovation knows no bounds.

3. **Myth:** The process of innovation is chaotic and unpredictable.
   Reality: The creative process can be unpredictable, but there are processes and systems that can be put into place to encourage it.

4. **Myth:** An innovation will always require millions of dollars of investment.
   Reality: Coming up with new products and concepts can be expensive, but some of the best have been on a shoestring.

5. **Myth:** Innovation is about producing wild-eyed ideas.
   Reality: Innovation is about taking the best ideas and executing them.

A Brief History of Innovation

Bold change produces wealth and creates jobs, and pushes the economy to new heights.

Creative thinking can lead to medical advances, saved lives, jobs, and more. But the process is not totally positive, which is why I think of it as a *Janus proposition.* Janus was the two-headed Greek god who could look both ways at the same time. Innovation is also two-headed: it is neutral in the sense that how we use it can either add or take away value. I cannot tell the whole history of innovation, but I can tell some snippets from history.

A school child in the United States learns something about the history of innovation by the 8th grade. Johannes Gutenberg was a goldsmith living in Germany in the 15th century. One day, in a drunken stupor, he tinkered with a wooden wine press until he got something that could be used with ink to print on paper—the first printing press. Besides being a painter, Leonardo da Vinci came up with the first designs for a helicopter and instruments of war, and was generally way ahead of his time. Robert Fulton designed a steamship, Elias Howe a sewing machine, and Jonas Salk penicillin. Henry Ford's most important innovation was mass production of automobiles using an assembly line. The Wright brothers, smart bicycle mechanics, are credited with inventing the first airplane that could fly. (Of course, because of lack of space, books fail to mention that the Wright brothers were unsuccessful getting off the ground 47 times before they succeeded.) The Curies discovered radiation (although both died of cancer). Surely you can expand this list of successful innovators.

The Oprah Innovation

Oprah Winfrey has just announced that she is ending her very popular television talk show after 25 years. This show has had provocative, famous, and interesting guests, and has spawned book groups throughout the country. What was her innovation? She showed that intimate, "private" subjects could be discussed on air, in front of millions of people. She showed that everyday people wanted to hear discussion about issues such as abortion, incest, rape, deformities, and genocide. Before Oprah's show, these issues were not discussed widely in the media.

Incidentally, media people are asking, "Who can be the new Oprah?" A more insightful question might be, "How can television networks innovate ever further?"

The Darker Side of Innovation

Then, there is the history of bad innovations that are supposed to create positive results. Most textbooks do not include these "good" ideas that had sinister consequences for somebody:

- The Romans cut the Achilles tendons of all the soldiers they conquered so the men would never be able to fight Rome again.

- The Nazis came up with innovative ways of killing thousands of people at the same time—by gassing them.

- Catholic priests in the Middle Ages made themselves wealthy by selling indulgences. Such money-making would make contemporary fundraisers green with envy.

- The Spanish conquistador Hernán Cortes landed his expedition near Veracruz, Mexico in 1519. After a short time of finding no riches but many mosquitoes, his men started grumbling about going home. To stop this line of thought, Cortes burned their five ships; "There is no going home, boys...." That creative solution increased the level of commitment among his men.

- Agent Orange was air-dropped on the forests in Vietnam so the Viet Cong would not be able to hide from American forces. It also caused cancer and birth defects in the people exposed to it.

- The atom bomb saved a half a million American lives by bringing Japan to its knees, but more than 200,000 Japanese were killed in the process.

- Research on animals has led to many medical breakthroughs, but large numbers of these monkeys and other animals are harmed or killed in the process.

- And of course there are efficient lobotomies, which remove dangerous brains.

Thus the dark side lurks in the shadows of many important innovations.

Try This!

1. What innovations have been put into place in your organization (concepts, products, etc.)?

2. How have they evolved or worked out over time?

Breakthroughs do not always come in the form of cardiac pacemakers or monkeys or napalm. Many of those innovations were on purpose; inventors set out to create a product for a specific task and were successful. Let us look at other ways that innovations happened.

Innovating by Accident

Many innovations emerge out of accidents. In fact, Mark Twain once called "Accident" the greatest of all inventors. Common sense tells us, however, that someone has to process what he or she sees or experiences, and then think through how to apply it to a specific problem. For instance, Eli Whitney watched a cat pull bird feathers through a birdcage. (Poor Tweety bird!) Now, many people have observed this same phenomenon, reflected on what the bird was doing, and thought nothing of it. Eli Whitney saw an idea of how to comb cotton mechanically. Much labor was saved at the expense of one little bird.

Many products are the result of accidents. Some of them are well known. A 3M scientist spilled some chemical on her new shoes, and it did not come off. Aha! Scotchgard was invented. Art Fry, another 3M researcher, learned about a glue that did not stick very well. He was in church one day, trying to keep his hymnal bookmarks from slipping out. He decided to see if the adhesive could be used for bookmarks. This idea led to the development of Post-it™ Notes. In 1928, Alexander Fleming left a window open next to a petri dish with a colony of bacteria. He looked through a microscope, but instead of seeing just another ruined experiment under the lens, he noticed that mold was destroying the bacteria. This led to the development of penicillin.

Then there was that French guy who got tired of pulling burrs off his hunting dog. Out of his irritation grew Velcro.

22

Blockbuster, Netflix, and Redbox

Many of us were delighted when a video store, say Blockbuster, came to our neighborhood. Saturday night and nothing to do? A quick run to the store and a home movie for the evening. Then, many couch potatoes and semi-invalids were even more excited with the advent of Netflix. We could now have videos delivered to our home, keep them for as long as we wanted, and then send for more, all for a low monthly cost. Netflix was able to keep the price reasonable by eliminating high rent store fronts and costly labor. Mail was much cheaper.

Redbox innovated even further—why not a vending machine, like soft drinks, and just route drivers? They reduced renting costs to one dollar per day and put their "redboxes" in MacDonald's and grocery stores and other popular places. They eliminated mailing costs and many of the labor costs. Their price points were significantly lower than Blockbuster's price of about four dollars a video.

Netflix went a step further; you can rent a video through a digital system that eliminates the mail system and, therefore, theoretically reduces costs. What is the next "disruptive" innovation? Will Blockbuster be knocked out? How about Netflix or Redbox?

Other accidental innovations are not as well known.

- Percy Lebaron Spencer, an American engineer at Raytheon who never finished grammar school, held 120 patents, mostly in the defense industry. One day, he walked by a machine used in radar called a magnetron and noticed that the candy bar in his pocket melted. Spencer grabbed a handful of popcorn kernels and put them in front of the magnetron—they popped! In 1945, he invented the microwave oven, which Raytheon later manufactured. There is now a building at Raytheon named after him.

- Pharmacist John Walker was mixing chemicals to produce a drug. Some of the mixture stuck to the mixing stick. Walker tried to scrape it off, and it burst into flames. He kept experimenting, calling the now-flammable sticks "sulphuretted peroxide strikables." Granted, the name of his invention needed a bit of refining: they are known as matches.

- Eleven-year-old Frank Epperson forgot about a mixture he made of soda powder and water and it froze to a mixing stick. Twenty years later, Epperson took his original idea and added some flavoring. Lo and behold, "Eppsicles." Again, the name needed some refinement. Those popsicles earned him royalties of 60 million dollars. His innovation, of course, became more than a food: it became a way of keeping hot and tired kids from getting too ornery.

- And let us all give thanks to Tim Berners-Lee, a British physicist and computer scientist, who was trying to figure out a way to organize his notes in order to keep track of his random ideas and thoughts. He is credited with inventing the World Wide Web. He was just being a self-centered researcher, yet his idea became the basis for something billions of people worldwide now rely on.

This small group of examples should force us all to ask one key question:

> *How can I refine my power of observation in order to see innovations instead of accidents, mistakes, or random occurrences?*

Innovating by Getting into a Different Box

Creativity theorists encourage people to "get out of the box." The theory is that while you are inside a self-imposed box, you will not invent anything new. So get out of that box!

An opposing theory, posed by Andrew Hargadon in *How Breakthroughs Happen,* suggests that getting out of the box is not as important as hopping into a different box. Hargadon believes that innovations and new technologies come from a confluence of people, ideas, and objects *from different boxes.* He says that innovators are not smarter, more creative, or stubborn than the rest of us. They are simply better connected to other individuals and groups who can help them execute.

It is about networks. Breakthrough innovations cause new networks to happen. Whole groups of people, ideas, and objects form new relationships overnight. These networks, the webs of significance we ourselves have spun, shape who we are and what we think. Hargadon calls these "networks of possible wanderings."

Let us look at some examples. For instance, the Internet is what it is because other innovations made it possible: computers, networking technologies, communication protocols, optical fiber, network servers, local networks, mail servers, modems, personal computers, and desktop applications such as e-mail and Web browsers. Another advanced technology—for its time—was the telegraph—the Internet of the Victorian Age. The first telegraph (1774) was a set of 26 conductors. New ideas about electricity and insulating wire were added. In 1837, Samuel Morse developed an "alphabet" code of dots and dashes. Then an operator was added. Thomas Edison developed ways to send messages further and faster. Clearly, without

26

the innovations developed and many years earlier, the Internet as we know it today would not exist.

Innovation in Thinking

Innovations do not just come in products and services. Several professors are trying to push the rest of us to think better and more clearly. Dan Ariel, in *Predictably Irrational*, shows us, through copious examples, how our thinking is often irrational and self-defeating. For example, he shows us how the word "free" often leads us to make suboptimal purchasing decisions. Cass Sunstein and Richard Thalyer, in *Nudge*, invite us to examine our thinking patterns. In specific, they make the distinction between "automatic" thinking and "reflective" thinking. Often, we use automatic thinking when we should be using reflective thinking and get ourselves into financial and other kinds of trouble. These innovations in thinking have led the authors to positions as advisors to President Obama.

Hargadon reminds us that invention is about common and uncommon connections and combinations. According to most textbooks, the steamship was invented by Robert Fulton in 1807. However, the original idea was proposed in 1543, and commercial efforts began in 1707. Over the next hundred years, many different people worked on the basic concept before Fulton came along and developed the winning design.

How about the Reebok Pump athletic shoe? One of its designers was known for once creating inflatable splints. Two others had previously worked on ideas for medical IV bags. Several others worked on designs for diagnostic instruments. The result: an inflatable air bladder with mini pumps, tubes, and valves! Two of the most famous combinations of previous inventions came from Thomas Edison and Henry Ford. Edison's electric lighting combined elements of the telegraph, the arc light, and the existing gaslight industry. Edison's mimeograph pen borrowed the mechanics of high-speed telegraph repeaters.

Henry Ford sent two of his top engineers to the stockyards in Chicago. They found that stockyards were processing pigs in an assembly-line fashion. The carcasses slid down the line and pieces were cut off and processed in sequence. Henry Ford allegedly stated: "What is good enough for pigs is good enough for cars." Soon afterward, assembly lines were born.

> **Resource**
> ***Innovation at the Verge***
> (Star Thrower Distribution, 2009,
> www.starthrower.com)
>
> *Innovation at the Verge* is a video written and produced by Joel Barker, Futurist, author, and educator. Joel Barker is known for popularizing the concept of paradigms for businesses. This video shows how many innovations emanate from the confluence of two ideas. For instance, gift bags emerged at the confluence of gift wrap and brown paper bags. This video pushes viewers to examine the verges around them. It gives viewers tools to use to build the innovation capacity in their organizations.

Innovating When You are Outside the Field

You don't have to be an expert in a specific field of inquiry to come up with a breakthrough. Consider these examples:

- The ballpoint pen was invented by a sculptor.

- The parking meter was invented by a journalist.

- The Wright brothers were bike mechanics, not aeronautical engineers.

- Kodachrome film was developed by a musician.

29

Sometimes researchers and engineers are so glued to existing systems and processes already in place that they fail to see new possibilities. Futurist Joel Barker calls this "being stuck in one's paradigm." Think of a paradigm as the set of rules of a given system—the way things work within that particular domain. People living in a defined paradigm accept the rules as they are. People outside the paradigm see the "world" differently, and are not bound by those same rules. Looking at the world they currently inhabit differently allows them to be more open to possibilities and innovation.

The First Step in Innovation

What is the first step in the process of innovation?

- Brainstorming? *Wrong.*
- Asking the customer? *Wrong.*
- Having a brilliant idea? *Close, but wrong.*
- Setting up a manufacturing site in China? *Wrong.*

What is the first step in innovation? All of the following: Forget. Unlearn. Destroy. Dismantle. Undo creatively. To innovate, you must get rid of the old.

An old story goes like this: An intelligent, rich man visited a wise guru at a monastery in India. "I want to be your student," he told the guru. "People have said that you are very wise." The Westerner went on to tell the guru about all of his accomplishments. The guru looked at him thoughtfully, and he offered the man tea. When the tea was brought in, the monk began to pour the tea. And he kept pouring the tea, even as it overflowed the cup. And he kept pouring, even as the rich man tried to intercede.

"You can't pour tea into a full tea cup," the rich man said. "Yes, I know," replied the guru. "But teaching you would be the same thing."

You cannot add more to an already full vessel. In order to make something new, you have to get rid of old forms. In order to create a new business process, you have to be ready to abandon the old process. That is why Jim Collins, author of *Good to Great*, taught us that good is the enemy of great. If something is working well, why change it? Leave good enough alone. You have to be willing to destroy, throw away, abandon, leave behind, or blow up the old before you go on to something new.

Try This!

Stop doing. To be innovative means letting go of the past and making space for the future. How can you do that?

1. What should be on your "stop doing" list? What are you doing regularly that is not adding value for anyone?

2. What processes (evening routines, weekend mornings, making dinner) are you stuck to? Which are you willing to give up in order to innovate?

3. What are you willing to get rid of in your life?

4. What are you willing to unlearn or forget? Often, to learn something new, one needs to unlearn something. Before we embrace the world as round, we need to let go of the belief that the world is flat. (I need to unlearn some things in order to improve my skills in cooking.)

5. What must you destroy, first, in order to create something new?

If you did not like the last story, here is another one to intrigue you, paraphrased from the writings of Karl Weick. It seems that in 1949, a group of 23 firefighters were fighting a runaway forest fire in the mountains of Montana. The wind changed direction, and the fire bore down on the smokejumpers. The fire chased them up the slope, but they refused to drop their heavy tools because they would need them to fight the fire. Unfortunately, the men could not outrun the flames. If they had dropped their tools, they might have made it to safety, but they had been trained to keep their tools with them and not let go of them. Sadly, 14 men died.

The first step of innovation is to let go. What are *you* afraid of letting go of? And by hanging on to that, what opportunities are you *not* taking?

After World War II, the Japanese began to improve their manufacturing processes and procedures. All of their major cities were bombed, so they were starting from scratch—from nothing. Japan embraced total quality management under W. Edwards Deming. It took decades for the United States to do the same. Why? Because we already had manufacturing in place, intact, that worked well enough to remain competitive in world markets. We did not understand the importance of starting from scratch.

This "letting go" is a difficult step. The trapeze artist must let go of one trapeze before being able to grab the next one. For an instant, she or he has

33

nothing to hold on to. For an entrepreneur, that "instant" might be for months or years. And sometimes, we need to be pried away from what is safe.

"Destroy, dismantle, unlearn, forget!" Perhaps this isn't the mantra you were expecting, but it is a requirement for innovative thinking.

Key Points

- The first step in the innovative process is to let go of the old—or at least be willing to do so.

- Innovation can be defined as the practical application of creative ideas.

- Innovators have been with us since some caveman chiseled out a wheel. Innovation occurs as a result of an accident, a dream, an intuitive flash, or a merging of two or more ideas.

- Innovations can be good (new medicines) or bad (gas chambers).

- Innovation can be fun! Think of yourself as a detective searching for solutions to pressing problems

- Most innovators are passionate about their work.

Innovate Your Life!

Do you innovate in your life? See how many of these statements are true for you.

- ❏ I attempt to regularly establish new friendships.
- ❏ I try new types of entertainment and food.
- ❏ I read magazines outside of my field.
- ❏ I am curious about how things work.
- ❏ I find new places in my community to visit.
- ❏ I like to scan new books at my local bookstore or library.
- ❏ I seek out interesting people to talk to.
- ❏ I am regularly trying to improve products and processes.
- ❏ I like to create interesting presents for friends and family.
- ❏ I know of ways to make the world better.

Chapter 2:
The Innovative Mind

"Our business needs a massive transfusion of talent, and talent, I believe, is most likely to be found among non-conformists, dissenters, and rebels."

– David Ogilvy, advertising pioneer

Here is a paradoxical question: Are innovators born or are they made?

Innovation is not an event—it is a mindset. So, what is the exact mindset of an innovator? There is no one answer. Two dashes of Gates, add a cup of Einstein, throw in a tablespoon of Ford, and simmer in Edison's lab for a couple years, and *voila!* You have a bona-fide, guaranteed innovator.

So what is the answer to my question? Are innovators *born,* or are they *made?* An astrologer might say that a person with their sun in Cancer and moon in Aries might have a better chance at being an innovator than one with, say, a sun in Virgo and moon in Scorpio. Psychologists might say that a person with a Myers Briggs of ENFP might be naturally a better innovator than an ISFJ. A psychologist might also look at birth order, or how dysfunctional the family of origin is, or at what age the child was toilet trained. A sociologist might look at the culture and ascertain whether or not it supports creativity. But there is no sure recipe.

Innovative Traits

Regardless of whether innovators are born or made, many of them have traits that push their creative abilities. Let us look at six specific abilities that many innovators have in common.

Curiosity. Innovators and creators are curious about their world. They look below the surface of life. They do not ignore gaps in their own knowledge, but explore these gaps and attempt to fill them. Why is the sky blue, but the river green? Why can't we administer drugs more safely? Why does the earth have to heat up so fast?

Let me tell you about one innovator I know who lives in the Seattle area. Roger has dozens of inventions under his belt. He has a radiant-heating device that is based on what is known about the eyes of the lobster. He was walking along the wharves of Seattle one day and started looking at the eyes of lobsters that had been unloaded from a fishing boat. How *do* they work, he asked himself. He tore through encyclopedias, trying to figure those eyes out, and used some of the principles he learned in the development of his heating devices.

Risk taking. Innovators are risk-takers—but when it is appropriate. I say "appropriate" because, contrary to myths, innovators often roll the dice. Some occasionally win. Walt Disney and George Macy went bankrupt multiple times before they created their business empires. In an incredible risk-taking episode, Fred Smith of FedEx reportedly gambled with his last $1,000 in Las Vegas in order to make payroll for his fledgling company. Most innovators are not reckless; they are thoughtful and rational. They are willing to put years of hard work into inventions that might or might not work out.

But at the root, they believe in themselves. Innovators are willing to gamble on their own ideas and schemes. Innovators often see the upside of their work long before they see the downside. Sometimes they see the upside unrealistically, but they still see an upside. Many of them are serial innovators who have failed and survived. So, failing is not such a downside after all.

Albert Einstein was not a normal little boy. Neither was the composer Mozart. In high school, Bill Gates snuck out of his house at one in the morning to use computers at a nearby university. Edgar Allan Poe was downright weird. Leonardo da Vinci followed around deformed people in

---

(continued)

order to sketch them (he would probably be arrested as a stalker these days). He also allegedly stole cadavers from the morgue to study. Face it, innovators are not usually normal. They are people with "weird" ideas. They look at the world differently. They do not sit quietly and obediently, with hands crossed, in Ms. Johnson's second grade class (unless they are creating imaginary worlds in their minds). They were problematic students, conducting dangerous experiments, replaying the Battle of Waterloo with Napoleon winning, or trying to text an Eskimo in the Arctic Circle.

Assumption challenging. We walk through life unaware of many of the assumptions that are embedded in our reality. We assume that automobiles must have four wheels, pens must use ink, colleges must have classrooms, etc. Innovators routinely question assumptions that others take for granted. Once upon a time, radios required large cathode ray tubes, and all cars had to run on gas. Now they do not. Once upon a time, you had to attend on-campus classes during the week in order to obtain a university degree. Not so any more. Now all of those assumptions have been challenged successfully. Who said people won't pay $4.00 for a cup of coffee? They will. Who said people won't pay to do volunteer work in another country? They will.

- For successful innovators, questioning assumptions is part of life. There can be large upsides to the process of assumption-testing. It can be annoying to others who are asked questions like "Why can't you put paprika on broccoli?"

- Innovation can save money. (Why can't that process be done in five steps, rather than in 12?)

- It can revolutionize industries. (Why can't music be downloaded from the Internet, saved, and played digitally instead of only being available on a CD?)

- A culture of innovation can make for a joyful and sane workplace. (Patagonia asked: Does work have to be oppressive and boring?)

- Innovation can create millionaires.

- Innovation can save lives. (Can river blindness in Africa be prevented?)

Change agent. Innovators are, by nature, change agents. Innovations change lives, change workplaces, change power relationships, and change perspectives. Innovators embrace change, and by their work, they push others to do the same. Art Fry of 3M made it possible for me to "evolve" by moving from paperclips to Post-it™ Notes. That shift does not radically change my life, but it does make doing work easier. Howard Schultz of Starbucks created a place for me to write books, away from the distractions of home and work. He changed the way I do work.

Change agents are not afraid of going up against the status quo. Martin Luther King wanted to change the status quo. So did Nelson Mandela. So did the creator of the Segway. But change agents are not always popular. In fact, often they are not popular because they rock the boat, and some people in the boat just do not like to be rocked. As change agents, these innovators are not afraid to explore new territory, but they usually have to drag others along, kicking and screaming, with them.

Expect the Unexpected

Percy Spencer did not expect the chocolate bar in his pocket to melt as he walked by the magnetron machine. Jonas Salk did not expect mold to grow in his Petri dish that he left by the window in his laboratory. Innovations are often preceded by anomalies. Innovators see anomalies where others see nothing.

Tolerance for ambiguity. Innovators can live with the unanswered question better than most of us. They tolerate the ambiguity of the unknown. Answers might not be readily available, but that is fine with them. They do not find the tension of "not knowing" to be either dangerous or unsettling. As a result, they can live at the fringe of processes, procedures, and ways of life, and see possibilities that others cannot see. This is the hallmark of an innovative mind.

Innovators know that every change will look like a failure at some point. They don't judge scary moments in between as failures (such as bankruptcy), but rather as possibilities. Tolerance for ambiguity is a great attribute to have in times of change. We do not know what lies around the corner, so in this way innovators are out ahead of most of us. During the invention and innovation process, they have learned to be patient about not being able to predict the outcome of their efforts.

> "You have to be open to the unexpected, so that if you come upon a discovery, you'll recognize it and act upon it." Stephanie Kwolek, chemist, *Fast Company*, April 2000.

Passion and joy. Some evidence suggests that innovators and creative types are long-suffering, unhappy people. A few, such as Virginia Woolf and Ernest Hemingway, end up committing suicide. Others, Edgar Allen Poe among them, drink themselves to death.

43

Actually, most innovators are joyful of their life. This emerges out of their passion for their work. Many authors and artists talk about the joy of practicing their craft, the long hours absorbed in their callings. Employees who work for such innovative companies as Patagonia, IDEO, and Ben and Jerry's often talk about the joy in their work. For most innovators, the excitement of creating something new blossoms into joy.

Persistence. Many successful innovators are serial failures. They go out of business, create things that do not work, and sell to the wrong markets. They squander money, use up friendships, stay up until the wee hours, are overfunded or underfunded, and are plagued by bureaucracy. And yet, they persevere. They keep walking uphill, through the snowstorm, against the wind, without boots. The 3M marketing department initially turned down Art Fry's Post-it™ Notes idea before the company was convinced it would be a hit.

Fill in the blank. What factors do *you* think are necessary for innovation? There are many other things that are helpful: being organized, having the ability to gather resources and support, and a deep and broad understanding of an industry.

Thinking Skills for Innovators

Strengthening thinking skills is critical for innovation. These skills are broad, and each deserves a book of its own. Would-be innovators should focus on developing and strengthening all of them.

The ability to think creatively. This one is obvious. You have to think outside of the box, and engage in lateral thinking. When you find your mind wandering down railroad tracks, you have to derail it and set off in a different direction. The mind needs to take a different perspective. Many "creativity" exercises are designed to take us off our current path and down a new one. A cook tries a different combination of spices. A parent puts together a surprising series of challenges for a birthday party. The author of a series of novels suddenly takes his readers into an exciting new world. Entertainment parks such as Disneyworld transport us to a creative fantasy world, filled with unexpected twists and turns.

Try This!

Develop your own creative capacity:

- Quickly write down 20 ways to use a brick.
- Ask 25 questions about the tree outside of your window.
- Read magazines outside of your field.
- Drive a different route to work today.
- Keep a journal of all the creative and innovative things you see.

Creative thinking is a complex set of skills that help us create something new. Here are six key skills:

- Fluency: the ability to generate many ideas quickly

- Flexibility: the ability to respond in a variety of ways to a variety of situations

- Originality: the ability to develop new and unique ideas

- Elaboration: the ability to build upon an existing idea

- Brainstorming

- Synthesizing: the ability to take two or more ideas and combine them into a third new idea

Creative thinking also draws on the ability to differentiate between ideas and evaluate them, use imagery and metaphor, get rid of bias, modify, make mental associations, and so on. If you develop all of these abilities, you will be a very powerful person. Of course, many of these characteristics are ideals. (Good luck, for instance, freeing yourself from internal biases. That is a lifelong spiritual goal for some of us!)

Creative people develop most of these abilities. I know a man who listed 120 uses of a brick in 10 minutes. Now that is fluency! Barnes and Noble's Bookstore has taken the old "we just sell books" and elaborated on it, and now we associate it with music, gifts, high-end chocolates, coffee, comfortable chairs, a meeting place, authors' readings, child-friendly reading areas, and so on. This is clearly not your grandfather's bookstore.

Systems Thinking

Today's competition is not between innovator and innovator, but innovative systems. Most innovations emanate from partnerships within and between organizations. For instance, think tanks, research laboratories, universities, and corporations often create partnerships in order to develop new innovations. Corporations are realizing that not all of the knowledge that they need resides in their own halls. They are striving to find the best creative combination of entities which will push forward innovations.

Peter Senge, author of *The Fifth Discipline,* refers to systems thinking as wide-angle vision, rather than telephoto vision, because it looks at the big picture and all of the interconnections rather than a narrow sliver of reality. Systems thinking is a way of looking at the world in which relationships, patterns, and interrelationships become primary. Several principles of systems thinking are important for innovators.

The Law of Unintended Consequences. Quick-fix solutions for problem symptoms often lead to other problems. The best way out of a hangover is another beer, but that will lead back into the original problem. The unintentional consequences of years of eating greasy fast-food might be gallstones and emergency gall bladder surgery. The increasingly common unintentional consequences of text messaging while driving are serious traffic accidents. The unintended consequences of spraying DDT on crops for pest control was the near annihilation of the majestic bald eagle in the United States.

What are the unintended consequences of your innovations? Will they create problems elsewhere? Will they have deleterious effects on other parts of your product line, and cannibalize other sales? We cannot always predict the unintentional consequences of an innovation, but we can look ahead and try to map them out. This discipline of identifying possible first-, second-, and third-order consequences can help us foresee future impediments.

Lag Variables. One systems truth says that *cause and effect are not related in time or space*—there are time and space lags. Advertise now and maybe get sales results in six months. Investing in research and development might not pay off for years. A nuclear accident like Chernobyl killed reindeer thousands of miles away, and created birth defects in children years later. My craving for sweets will create dental problems for me many years down the road. Policies made in Washington today will have implications for people in rural Afghanistan for years to come.

Innovators need to give themselves time to experiment. They must have patience, because their innovations are not likely to be readily accepted. Many artists and inventors were unknown during their own lifetime; what they were trying to accomplish was not apparent for decades after they died. Innovators in art and science, but also in business, are often way ahead of their time. The rest of the world often needs time to catch up.

Creative people have much to learn from previous innovators about the spread or acceptance of an idea or new product. Often, that data is available. But more important, we need to understand that

49

the world does not always work in a linear, cause-and-effect fashion. Instead, the effect part might come years later or in an unexpected place. Innovators must embrace mystery: they might never know how things turn out.

An ability to notice events, patterns, and structures. Many people go through life with an "event" orientation. Here an isolated event, there an isolated event. Innovators, on the other hand, must look past the superficiality of events to the pattern beneath events, and to the structure that is creating the patterns. Isolated events in my life were a broken finger, a pulled muscle, and a black eye during consecutive soccer games. I looked at them just as events, yet there was a pattern: these injuries happened every Sunday when I played goalie. What was the underlying structure creating this pattern? I was a 47-year-old playing with 22-year-olds. Injury was a high likelihood.

I once had a boss whose wife would call in sick for him on a regular basis. This happened mostly on Mondays (the pattern). The structure? He would drink too much on weekends and hadn't had time to recover by Monday.

Opportunities can be found when looking at patterns and structures. Decades ago, General Motors noticed that farmers were tearing the back seats out of their cars in order to carry big things.

Someone thought about this and said to his boss, "Let's build a pick-up." A few plastic manufacturers noticed that toddlers spill their milk; "How about a cup with a top?" The sippy cup was born.

Problems and Symptoms. Products and services on the market often solve symptoms, rather than problems. Headaches, for example, are often symptoms of neck or shoulder stress. Aspirin helps the short-term pain, but what will treat the real problem that causes the headaches? Many research dollars over the past 50 years have been funneled into finding cures to cancer. But some innovators are looking hard at the principles of social psychology in order to identify lifestyle changes that will *prevent* cancer.

Creative thinkers look at major problems and see that only the symptoms are being treated. Addressing the *real* problems can reap large profits and help numerous people, but it will require the brain of a detective and an inquiring mind. The first step, again, is a change of mindset; what is the problem, and what is the problem-symptom?

The ability to see connections. Systems-thinking is about seeing connections and interrelationships. Can there be a connection between coffee shops and bookstores? Is there a connection between driving an SUV and icebergs melting? How about a

Romanian orphanage and a childless family in Chicago? I can guarantee that there are connections between some of my great grandfather's attitudes toward woman and my own, unfortunately.

According to Thomas Friedman, ours is an increasingly connected world. As Friedman wrote in his book, *The World is Flat,* the components for your Dell Computer originate in 13 different countries. Seeing connections before others notice them can yield large results and profits, and many multinational companies see just that.

Emotional Intelligence

Psychologist Daniel Goleman's research suggests that 85% of a person's success in life is due not to mental intelligence, but to their *emotional intelligence.* Creative people know that they must work through other people to make their innovations marketable or usable. They also need to understand themselves better: their priorities, values, moods, work cycles, and their own trigger points. Emotional intelligence encompasses many traits. Let us examine several important ones.

Self-understanding. The platform upon which much of our emotional intelligence rests is self-awareness or self-understanding. Here's one question that I ask all of my clients: "How are you 'showing up' in the world?"

Sounds like an easy question, right? Not really. Many people do not know how they come across to others. Some appear depressed, angry, sullen, aloof, or agitated, and often do not realize it. I once worked with someone who was constantly angry. People just did not want to be around him. I know another person who is constantly sullen and unhappy, and she has no idea that people try to avoid her. These moods can be off-putting to others.

Innovators have to sell their ideas to others. How they come across to others is often the margin between success and failure. At the very least, an innovator needs to be self-confident, rather than tentative, doubtful, or just plain aloof.

The road to self-awareness can be tough, but is usually very rewarding. Obtaining feedback from trusted others is one way of becoming more self-aware. *"How did I come across in that meeting? Was I too aggressive?"* Participating in twelve-step groups and therapy groups is another way to raise one's self-awareness. Watching one's moods and triggers, taking deep breaths, and giving yourself moments of reflection can also reveal patterns of emotional states.

Many inventors and innovators are known for their low EQ or emotional intelligence. Stories abound about innovative company presidents who have temper tantrums and berate their employees. Books about inventors create a myth that creative folks are antisocial eccentrics who expect others to walk around on eggshells around them. Innovators who make or save millions may get away with this type of behavior, but most of us mortals cannot. The world will eventually walk away from difficult people.

Trigger Points. Most of us suffer some pain in childhood, and those pools of pain remain with us, sometimes throughout our entire lives. Other people's words and actions can trigger them. For instance, receiving a parking ticket might make some people think, "How can I waste money like that? I am bad." I have a pool of pain around a fear that no matter what I do, it is not enough. So, when I make an elaborate meal and a child says "Can I have a bagel, dad?" that pool of pain is activated. A friend of mine who never had children can't sit behind small children at church without triggering her "no children" pool of sadness.

Trigger points can send us into sadness, depression, anger, or shame, or conversely into joy, comfort, or happiness. (When I hear the rock band, the Grateful Dead, I fondly reminisce about driving my truck around Montana as a teen.) An innovator needs to be self-aware enough to know when he or she is falling into a nonproductive stage, and be able to reverse it. If certain people trigger thoughts or emotions that reduce our productivity by taking us into moments of depression or sadness, we must avoid those people. It behooves innovators to know their own emotional trigger points.

Assumed Constraint. A circus elephant is put on a ten-foot chain attached to a stake for the first year of its life. After that, the chain is exchanged for twine. The elephant will still not go more than ten feet from the stake. The elephant is limited by an assumed constraint, believing that the chain is still holding it in place.

People are not much different—we assume constraints that are not always entirely accurate, such as these:

- I cannot garner enough resources to get this product to the market.

- Management will never support launching this new product.

- I am not smart enough to write a book.

- I am not experienced enough to make a contribution in that industry.

- There is not enough time to innovate effectively.

These constraints have been shattered by a variety of people and organizations. Innovators are the ones shattering these constraints.

Resilience. One of the key traits of an emotionally intelligent person is resilience. The human condition is one of failure and adversity. It is not about getting knocked down; it is about how fast you are able to get back up.

Try to figure out what these numbers mean: 6, 7, 22, 47, 128, 903, 1,330. Give up?

- 6 = number of times Walt Disney went bankrupt before he made it.

- 7 = number of times George Macy went out of business before he was successful.

- 22 = number of publishers who rejected Dr. Seuss's first book.

- 47 = number of times the Wright brothers did not get off the ground.

- 128 = number of short stories Ernest Hemingway wrote before one was published.

- 903 = number of light bulbs designed by Edison's team that did not work.

- 1,330 = number of times that Babe Ruth struck out in his career.

Inventors and innovators have to be resilient, because first efforts rarely succeed (nor do the second ones).

So, do you fold up after a failure, or do you get up and move on? In some ways, this might be the most important emotional intelligence trait for an innovator.

Like all of the emotional intelligence skills, resilience **is** a thinking skill. While some people put thinking and emotions into separate realms, they are often intertwined. Our thoughts determine our level of resilience. What we tell ourselves about adversities and failures determine our future actions. If we fail a math test and tell ourselves that we are bad in math, that experience will probably set our destiny when it comes to the world of numbers.

Self-Motivation. Individuals who are unmotivated are not likely to come up with creative or original ideas. Innovation requires change and shaking up the apple cart; people with a status-quo orientation are not typically innovative. Innovators tend to be self-starting and self-motivated. They also must be comfortable with delayed gratification. The fruits of their labors do not come readily; usually a time lag occurs. Many innovations, if not most of them, require patience and many renditions (e.g., Edison and light bulbs). Remember that Earl Bakken, inventor of the first wearable pacemaker, worked out of his garage for seven years before seeing some of the fruits of his labors.

Beyond delaying gratification, innovators need to be optimistic. Optimists see setbacks as little bumps; pessimists see obstacles as permanent or long term. Innovators are optimists in that they need to believe in their own talents and in their abilities to have an impact on the world. They wake up with self-motivation and confidence that they will be able to succeed in a world that will allow for successful innovation.

Relationship Management. The myth about the "Lone Ranger" innovator does not work in our complex world. Yes, a crotchety, annoying inventor or innovator might be successful, but only if she or he has someone to run interference and navigate relationships. After an idea is hatched, product designers, accountants, manufacturing engineers, marketers, and salespeople have to push it into the marketplace. These people need to be sold, nurtured, brought along, communicated with, and kept in the loop. The innovator needs to consciously build relationships with these individuals, because they constitute as much of a success factor as the "great idea." Some innovators (e.g., Picasso) can work almost in a vacuum, but many musicians and other artists employ handlers to take care of the relationship-management part. Most creative people have to work within the bounds of organizations, with all of their constraints, departments, and personalities. Innovators need to play nice in the sandbox in order to be effective!

Critical Thinking

Critical thinking is not about being critical and judgmental of other people. It means developing a critical eye for information and knowledge, and knowing how to use those precious commodities. *What do we know, and what do we not know?* is a central question for critical thinkers. What are the *gaps* in our knowledge? Critical thinking entrepreneurs are always looking for gaps—gaps in product offerings, gaps in service needs, and gaps in available information. *There might be a market there* is not good enough to warrant putting years and millions of dollars into a product.

A corollary of this principle is to differentiate between observation and inference. How are our minds filling in the gaps of what we do not directly observe? For instance, it didn't occur to anyone that millions of people might frequent coffee shops that served high-quality coffee. Howard Schultz, the founder of Starbucks, thought they would. And he was right.

Most people do not seem to be good critical thinkers. As individuals, we fall into a variety of thinking traps, many conditioned in us as children. The first step in improving our critical thinking

skills is to recognize our flaws, our gaps, our dysfunctional thinking. Then, we will be able to recognize it when our thinking goes awry and we fall into
suboptimal patterns of thinking. We can only cor-
rect ourselves when we are aware of what we are
doing. This process requires feedback from others.

Innovators must continuously evaluate their
ideas. The innovator who developed the concept of
combining a bowling alley with a movie theater
failed to assess the function of sound in each. The
founders of a nationwide donut chain did not criti-
cally assess the forces against obesity. *Does this
work? Is this really marketable? Can manufacturing
really build these rapidly?* If not, innovators will
waste much valuable time.

Key Points

- An innovative mindset requires four sets of
  abilities and skills: creative thinking; systems
  thinking; emotional intelligence; and critical
  thinking.

- There are many ways to strengthen these areas.
  Fortunately, they can be developed at most
  stages of life.

- An individual with an innovative mindset is
  curious, risk taking, passionate, persistent,
  assumption-challenging, and tolerant of ambiguity. He/she is also a change agent.

Resource
A Whole New Mind

Read Daniel Pink's *A Whole New Mind*, published by The Penguin Group in 2006. Pink, a writer by training, suggests that work requiring left-brained thinking will be done by computers in countries with lower labor costs. Pink argues that the youth of the Western world should be educated for the work of tomorrow in six different ways:

Design. Today, it is economically crucial and personally rewarding to create something that is also beautiful, whimsical, or emotionally engaging.

Story. The essence of persuasion, communication, and self-understanding has become the ability to also fashion a compelling narrative.

Symphony. What's in greatest demand today isn't analysis, but *synthesis*—seeing the big picture and crossing boundaries, and combining disparate pieces into an arresting new whole.

Empathy. What will distinguish those who thrive from those who do not will be their ability to understand what makes their fellow humans tick, their ability to forge relationships, and their care for others.

(continued)

Play. There is need for play in our work and personal lives. The current younger generation has been brought up on computer simulations, and learns well in that mode.

Meaning. We can pursue more significant desires: purpose, transcendence, and spiritual fulfillment.

Chapter 3:
The Innovative Culture

"My experience with innovation in organizations is probably similar to those of others. The leadership wants innovation, begs for innovation, and sets up committees to create innovations. Explicitly, organizations are very much in favor of innovation. Yet, when employees try to be innovative, corporate bureaucracies, policies and procedures, and red tape often squelch many innovative efforts. Like ping pong balls, creative innovators bounce between assessment committees, entrenched interests, quality task forces, and teams of nay-saying accountants. Bruised and beaten, they lick their wounds and 'stick to their knitting'."

– Richard Brynteson

Imagine an organization where employees take risks without fear of reprisal, and are encouraged to daydream and engage in creative brainstorming for hours. Imagine a room where all kinds of materials are readily available for tinkering. Imagine an organizational culture where innovation is a high priority. Imagine a playful, low-stress environment where people love to work.

For innovation to thrive, it has to become part of the DNA of an organization. Sadly, many companies relegate innovation to a few people over in product development. A truly innovative culture requires much more. In this chapter, we will look at how to create this kind of organizational culture.

Characteristics of an Innovative Culture

No two innovative cultures are alike, and there is no recipe or formula that will get you one. Several factors, however, are characteristic of organizations that support innovation. These attributes fall into two categories: psychological characteristics and physical characteristics. We will start by looking at the psychological environment of the organization.

"Failing Forward"

In an innovative culture, failing and learning from failure are encouraged. Risk taking and experimentation is encouraged. Following clues that lead to new territories is encouraged. As we have seen, the lives of entrepreneurs and innovators over the ages are littered with failures. Painters whose work goes unnoticed, bankrupt business owners, and inventions that no one wants are proof that the road to innovation is not all iPod-like success. Many end up as dead ends.

An innovative environment is one in which mistakes are encouraged and welcomed. In the early days of Apple Computer, Steve Jobs allegedly told his managers, "You are going to have to try new things, because we are growing so fast. I do not care if those things fail. Just change them if they do fail." The old ways of doing things do not work anymore. New things need to be attempted on a consistent basis in order for the organization to move forward, because many initiatives will fail. If those who try new processes or procedures are punished for failing, people will stop experimenting, creating, and modifying. Why take the risk?

Idea Killers

"We tried that 23 years ago and it did not work."

"I built that system myself—18 years ago."

"Our competition hasn't introduced that product. Why should we?"

"That product will never fit our margin guidelines."

"Leave the innovations to the product development people."

"We are going to table it for now, but keep thinking."

"Does it really fit with our core mission?"

"That wouldn't fit in our accounting system."

The other part of this "failing forward" equation is the forward part. Thomas Edison did not give up after 900 failed light bulbs. He allegedly said, "I now know 900 ways *not* to make a light bulb." He learned from those mistakes. One large computer company had a black book that documented errors that the company committed on previous projects. They regularly read the errors aloud and laughed at themselves. In this way, they reduced the likelihood of committing the same errors over again.

Yes, and. . .

"Yes, but..." is a common-yet-poisonous phrase. Yes, it is a good idea, *but we have no budget for something like that.* Yes, it is a good idea, *but it would never work here.* Yes, it is a good idea, *but management would never buy into it.*

A culture of innovation changes "Yes, but" to "Yes, and." It is a subtle change that renders large results. "Yes, but" ends a conversation and kills a subject. "Yes, and" encourages people to find ways to make something happen. It invites others to build on an idea. Training employees to say "Yes, and" may seem foolish, but it is one step forward in creating an innovative culture.

A Challenge-Based Culture

In an innovative culture, employees are expected to challenge assumptions and question the status quo.

A fear-based culture does not allow those practices. In some organizations, it is political suicide to continually ask questions like these:

- Why does that process take 14 steps?

- Why are we using aluminum in that product?

- Why is the sales force structured that way?

- Why do we have to fill out that form?

In innovative cultures, these questions lead to cost savings, efficiencies, and innovations. Innovators challenge the industry orthodoxies. They eat sacred cows. They test assumptions ruthlessly. They ask "Why?"

Take the insurance industry, for example. If you wanted to buy insurance years ago, you had to arrange for a rep to come to your house, take down two hours of data, and then get back to you in a month or so with a quote. Now, you can go online and fill out the information, submit it, and have an estimate in about ten minutes. You can also get comparative quotes from other insurance companies.

What factors are important in a culture that encourages people to challenge the status quo?

1. It must be a **trust-based culture.** Employees must trust that they will not be punished for challenging a way of doing things or questioning an existing policy or even the ideas of their superiors. People have to trust that management

67

will see such challenges in the light of an innovative spirit that welcomes the clash of ideas.

2. It must be a **high-dialogue culture.** Employees must be trained in how to discuss and debate ideas fully, building on each other and constructing the truth creatively. Ideas are built on and worked with, rather than attacked and destroyed. Instead of a right/wrong culture, it is a culture with many owners of partial truths. Discussions are used for bridging and adding, not staged as battles where there will be winners and losers.

3. It must be **a flat culture where hierarchies are not entrenched,** and where the ideas of management and employees combine and combust freely. Great ideas rarely flow from employees who do not believe that they are considered part of the team. In the most innovative companies, committees and task forces are composed of people from many levels of the organization, not just the top. Ideas are welcomed from all cracks and corners of the organization.

Some messages stifle innovation. "Bill," a top manager of a Midwestern organization, often frowned when he met with his employees. They took his frowning to mean that he was displeased. That signal cut short productive conversations. Bill was once asked why he frowned so much. He was not frowning he explained; he was just closing his mouth to hide his decaying teeth. The story does make us wonder about the messages we are sending. In what ways do managers subtly put down ideas in your organization?

Physical Environment

Physical structures can help or hinder a spirit of innovation. The comic strip *Dilbert* pokes fun at the uncreative landscape of cubicle hell, where employees are trapped in stuffy cubicles, told what to do and how to do it, and are given no opportunity to express their innovative spirit. In fact, the environment all but kills their spirit. Most people can tell stories about stifling environments where one needs five signatures to go to the bathroom.

What about innovative spaces? What do they look like? Playful and original physical spaces are often conducive to creativity. At Design Logic, a medical device product-development firm in Minneapolis, employees create their own cubicle space. Design Logic's offices are located in an old warehouse. The employees create the space while the company creates products. The company thus has an organic feel. Ideo, another product-design firm, encourages employees to create their workspace to match their working style.

Some organizations have created innovation rooms. The Innovation Office at the Singapore Department of Defense redesigned a room at the department's headquarters for ideation. The room has movable furniture, walls lined with flipcharts, and closets filled with everything from toys to materials (pipe cleaners, play dough, Legos, popsicle sticks) for prototype creation. The Department of Defense has an annual innovation contest with cash prizes. Any group can use this room in their innovation pursuits.

Other organizations build fun into their daily routines with Nerf basketballs or putting areas. Others sponsor exercise and yoga classes, and still others have their own on-site fitness centers. Physical movement during the day helps mental functioning as well as creative and innovative thinking.

Much innovation happens at "watering holes"— spaces where people gather informally during the day. A good example of this is the employee cafeteria at the specialty chemical company Ecolab in Mendota Heights, Minnesota. In the 1980s, the research facility there was a standard, perfunctory, drafty place with plastic chairs and a linoleum floor. There was no plush and comfortable ambiance, and no designer coffee. Yet at 9:30 a.m. most mornings, the chemists and scientists would start congregating here with their coffee. They talked about projects, experiments that worked and did not work, new ideas for products, and cutting-edge equipment. Sometimes, the "break" went on for 45 minutes. One or two executives complained about these elongated coffee breaks, but as a marketing manager at Ecolab, I found these gatherings as fascinating and innovative as any I have observed. They were exciting interchanges; ideas sparked, were built upon, were redirected, were sliced and diced, and were sent on flights of fancy.

> **Resource**
> *Innovation to the Core*
> by Peter Skarzynski and Rowan Gibson
>
> It is probably the best book written on how to create an innovative culture. The authors examine organizational cultures where innovation has taken hold, and show how organizations can leverage their own workforces to produce, care for, and turn ideas into marketable products and services. The book systematizes the process of innovation.

Organizational Structures

In the 1980s, organizations realized that some of their bureaucratic structures were too thick and regimented to allow for radical innovation. Embedded budget and reporting structures inhibited people from experimenting and trying to create something new. Product design teams were relocated to warehouses or basements off site, given autonomy and their own budget, and told to create. Tracy Kidder's book, *The Soul of a New Machine,* profiled a group of young employees from a computer company who were sent to a warehouse to develop a new computer. General Motors's Saturn division was given a similar mandate: employees were given acreage in Tennessee, far away from the stodgy confines of the GM bureaucracy, and told to build a totally new line of cars.

Another approach is to incorporate innovative structure within an existing organization. 3M, a Minnesota manufacturer and distributor of adhesives and other products, creates innovation "enhancers." Innovation clubs, roundtables, circles, and awards are all funded at 3M. A museum about innovation was created at 3M's corporate headquarters. Scientists who produce winning products like Post-it Notes and Scotchgard are given opportunities to do cutting-edge research. In fact, the company allows many researchers to allocate up to 15% of their time to work on projects of their choosing. The company mandates that 20% of revenue must come from products developed over the previous five years. There are many other structures at 3M that encourage innovation.

How do you eat an elephant? According to the children's joke, one bite at a time. Well, you change a culture the same way: one person, one initiative, one committee, one action at a time. Changing culture is a difficult process, but worth it. The rewards, monetary and nonmonetary, can be enormous. Besides, it might be the best survival tactic there is.

Creativity Killers

Dr. Theresa Amabile of Harvard University wrote that the three main determinants of creativity are expertise, creative thinking skills, and motivation. She suggests that of these three, motivation is the easiest to influence by managers. She writes of six distinct ways to influence motivation:

- *Challenge:* matching right person to right job with just enough challenge
- *Freedom:* freedom to pick the means to achieve a work goal
- *Resources:* Enough time and money to accomplish task—but not too much
- *Work-group features:* diversity with a common language
- *Supervisory encouragement:* innovators need cheerleaders, too
- *Organizational support:* information sharing, political help.

(Dr. Teresa Amabile, "How to kill creativity." *Harvard Business Review*, September/October, 1998)

73

Open-Source Innovation

Are all of the best and brightest research and development people available today currently employed
at your organization? Might there be excellent people elsewhere? Organizations across the country
have been asking themselves those two questions
in recent years, and are now looking outside their
hallowed walls for solutions. Proctor and Gamble,
the innovative consumer goods company in Cincin-
nati, stated recently that 50% of their new products
will come from outside the company.

Consider this story from *Wikinomics,* by Dan
Tapscott. In the 1990s, a gold mining company in
Canada had fallen on bad times. Its CEO took a sab-
batical and spent part of it at MIT, where he heard
about the open-source software operating system
Linux. He wondered if open-sourcing might work in
mining, traditionally a very secretive industry. He
decided to give it a try. He had all of the company's
research data put on the Internet, and offered
prizes for people who could find gold. Over 1,000
people took part in the contest, including miners,
graduate students, mathematicians, and former
soldiers. Some found gold. The company became very
successful, and over $500,000 in prize money was
awarded. Open-sourcing clearly worked for them.

Open-sourcing makes sense. Once upon a time,
information was closely held; it was a source of
power. Back in the Middle Ages, monks were the

teachers because they were the only people who could read and write. They held a virtual monopoly on written information. In our time, however, information is a commodity, freely distributed on the Web. Obscure information, once proprietary or buried in libraries, is now fairly easily accessed. People across the globe can access the same information and create together. The Internet started this process; online communities such as Facebook and MySpace and co-creation software continue to give this process wings. Here is another way of looking at it: The manufacture of complex products such as computers and cars is spread out across countries and companies. Why shouldn't co-creation also be so distributed?

Wikipedia, the online open-source encyclopedia, is the model for this type of co-creation. Thousands of contributors have added articles for this Website, and it now eclipses *Encyclopedia Britannica* as an information source for users of all ages. Because of the democracy of sourcing, errors are made, but they are corrected when detected. *Wikipedia* has added editing controls because of some attempts at sabotage, but the result is irrefutable: open-sourcing can help us create and innovate.

Open sourcing has come a long way in the telecommunications world. For instance, osalt.com is an open source software alternative. That website has access to many open source software products that all like commercial brands like iTunes and

Photoshop. The Open Handset Alliance touts itself as a "group of 65 technology and mobile companies" coming together in order to offer consumers less expensive handset applications. They have created "Android," an open and free mobile platform. These organizations exemplify what is possible in the world of open sourcing.

Leadership and the Innovative Culture

In 1912, Sir Earnest Shackleton and his 27-man expedition set out by ship for Antarctica. The ship became stuck in ice and could not move from the icepack for over 450 days. Innovation and optimism kept the men from starving, going mad, or becoming violent. Their dire straits necessitated using every resource available in novel ways. Many arctic expeditions ended in death and disaster. Despite extreme odds against their survival, not one of Shackleton's men died.

Leadership makes all the difference in an innovation initiative. Let us now look at why this is so.

Leadership factor #1: Communication. Employees are constantly looking for direction from their leaders. The better leaders are at communicating the priority of innovation, the more likely it will become part of that organization's culture. Communication comes through press releases, internal newsletters, speeches, and informal comments. Occasional lip service doesn't cut it—it relegates innovation to "flavor of the month" status.

An excellent example of leadership communication has been Jeffrey Immelt, who took over as CEO of General Electric from the legendary Jack Welch. He has set out two priorities for General Electric: innovation and green. Through all forms of communication, oral and written, he has instilled in that organization that innovation is extremely important for their profits.

Leadership factor #2: Reward systems. Employees typically do what they are paid to do. If reward systems favor the status quo, then employees will not rock the boat with new innovations. If compensation systems reward people for challenging the status quo and creating new systems and products, those behaviors will be encouraged. Likewise, if individual contributions are compensated, employees will focus on individual metrics. If, on the other hand, team efforts (from which most innovation occurs) are rewarded, an organization will see more team efforts.

Leadership factor #3: Vision. Leaders create and execute the vision and make sure everyone shares that same vision so it becomes reality. Is innovation a vital part of that vision? If not, an organization will not honor it as such.

77

Leadership factor #4: Attention. Do the top leaders stay aware of innovation efforts? Does the CEO check on the Research and Development team's work or pop in on process-redesign meetings? Or are innovation efforts treated as an afterthought? In order for innovation to become part of the DNA of an organization, the leadership has to push it as a necessity, as a part of day-to-day activities, and as a vital part of the organization's ongoing success. Nothing less will do.

Examples of Innovative Leadership

Governors Tim Pawlenty of Minnesota and Jim Doyle of Wisconsin worked together to figure out how Wisconsin and Minnesota could combine forces to create cost efficiencies at a time of extreme financial hardship. Each of these governors saw their budget woes getting more serious, so they took unique and innovative action together. This was innovative leadership, and both states benefitted from the cost savings.

Other leadership in innovation is legendary. Jeff Immelt shifted General Electric's focus from Six Sigma and cost efficiencies to "innovation" and "becoming green." Patagonia's founder Yves Chouinard encourages employees to create prototypes and try them out themselves. The leadership of Intel decided to build plants for the next generation of computer chips, even though the world is in the grips of a major recession.

78

Other CEOs channel money into other pockets to aid fledgling initiatives. For instance, at a Midwestern specialty chemical company, a couple of managers saw a market possibility for a new pool-cleaning service. They moved a few people into the enterprise quietly, and funneled money into it from several different sources as they tested the services and tried out several business models. They successfully kept the project under the radar from senior leadership while they nurtured it into success. After they had tweaked the model to make it profitable, they introduced the concept to the management of the company and to the marketplace.

Leadership Theorists and Innovation

Many leadership scholars point to directions that leadership should take in order to promote an innovative culture. James Kouzes and Barry Posner posit five leadership keys in their classic book *The Leadership Challenge.* One is to challenge the process—often one of the first steps in innovation. According to these authors, leaders must look at the status quo with new eyes. They must initiate the destruction of "the way things are" in favor of "the way things could be."

Harvard professor and author Ron Heifetz suggests that a leader's job is to make followers uncomfortable, rather than comfortable. The leader must challenge, push, and prod employees to do things that they would not otherwise do. The leader must also actively discourage complacency as a way of being. Such a belief system will be more likely to lead to innovation than being a nice leader who does not demand as much from his/her subordinates.

The Concept of Scaffolding

Scaffolding is a term that has been popularized in the field of education. It refers to a series of mechanisms that ensure the success of students. In order for students to understand an extremely complicated concept, they must be provided with "scaffolding." To grasp calculus, for example, students will need to have a foundation in algebra. In order to understand British Literature, they must have first studied the English language.

Teachers understand what students know and do not know. If a student is sure that the world is flat, teaching them that the world is round is not going to stick. The teacher has to first deconstruct or successfully challenge the notion that the world is flat. Only then will a student be open to the concept that the world is round.

Scaffolding in education also involves support and modeling—ensuring the success of the individual or the group. For instance, if a college is going to accept underprepared students in order to ensure an ethnic balance, the college needs to be able to provide tutoring, remedial classes, and mentoring for those students. Some colleges provide reading courses because some students' reading skills upon admission are inadequate. Other colleges provide peer-tutoring centers and writing centers. These mechanisms are built in to ensure student success.

How do you use scaffolding to create a culture of building innovation? Let us look at some important strategies.

If a CEO realizes the importance of innovation, he is going to order his top managers to be more innovative. They will agree, and when they get back to their office, they'll scratch their heads, wondering where to start. They might order their product development people to invent five new products. They might hire a guru to give a one-day workshop on being more innovative, or plan innovation "roundtables." Many of these initiatives are bound to fail, because there is no context, no support, or no scaffolding.

The concept of scaffolding can be used to build an organization's capacity for innovation. For innovation initiatives to be successful, the organization must provide the support, training, and a culture that encourages innovation. Let us look at some of the activities that can help build scaffolding for innovation.

Culture. Innovative thinking cannot survive in a highly undisciplined culture. Non-rule-abiding mavericks might get more attention than highly

81

disciplined people, but the disciplined people tend to come up with more original ideas and develop more products. Don't confuse bureaucracies with highly disciplined cultures. Bureaucracies have multiple layers, process forms, review boards, and controls *that do not add value*. Highly-disciplined cultures have few layers, and those only process forms, review boards, and controls *that add value* to processes. They have processes and systems that aid innovation, rather than discourage it.

For instance, in a bureaucratic culture, a review board will look for ways that an innovation *cannot* work in the current organization. In a highly disciplined culture, a review board will recognize a promising idea, and look for ways to apply an idea—or change a system so it *can* work. A bureaucratic culture will have antiquated controls in place that no one is willing to change. A disciplined culture, on the other hand, constantly evaluates its controls. A bureaucratic organization with a rigid 15% margin cut-off for all new products rather than a 15% guideline will miss out on some very innovative opportunities.

Ultimately, an innovative culture is one that teaches many ways to say "yes" to an interesting proposition, rather than "no" or "yes, but" or "interesting—let's ponder this." That kind of thinking has to be part of a deliberate, concrete, conscious, top-down philosophy.

Motivation. Managers in organizations have a variety of ways to encourage creative thinking and get people motivated. Many believe that extrinsic motivation is the most helpful form of motivation— $500 for a winning idea, for instance. Research in the field, on the other hand, suggests that *intrinsic* motivators are more powerful. Many companies have found it profitable to use a variety of forms of intrinsic motivation to spur innovation: research roundtables, awards, innovation circles, an innovation museum, and/or time off for innovation research.

Training in Processes. Training in processes helps organizations innovate in two ways.

1. When employees at several levels in the organization learn how to use process tools, such as flow charts and Gantt charts (a project-management tool used to sequence steps in a process), they become educated in how to improve existing processes. Task forces can reduce a nine-step process to five steps, which reduces cycle time, cuts costs, and helps customer relationships. These process tools are not rocket-science complex; they are logical, simple procedures that can be employed at any level in an organization.

83

2. Process tools can help build seamless systems for developing and evaluating new products and services. They can help expedite, rather than hinder, product development. Product development is really a series of stages: ideation; concept development; bench testing; and market analysis. Each step can be done efficiently with process tools. In this way, the organization does not have to reinvent the wheel every time someone develops another product or service.

Try This!

Creating a culture of innovation begins with a simple step. Hold a brown-bag discussion group about innovation, or have participants read the same book, or distribute an innovation article for participants to read and think about.

Talk about how to build innovation into your organization—there's no telling where these ideas will go.

Strengthening Emotional Intelligence. Emotional intelligence is essential for effective collaboration, because the innovative process requires effective communication and collaboration between departments. Close collaboration is directly dependent on people with high emotional intelligence. Timelines are compressed, departments rub against each other, and tempers flare when organizations try new things. Managers and employees need to have a high level of self-awareness and self-control if they are to weather the fierce winds of outside and inside forces. People need to know their own limits and boundaries, and need to show empathy for people from other parts of the system who are also under pressure. Emotional intelligence is a scaffold that needs to be built.

Lac Su and Nick Tasler authored a paper for TalentSmart entitled "EQ and Innovation," in which they suggest that engineers, especially, need to strengthen their own emotional intelligence because they must be able to connect not only with other engineers, but also with professionals outside their department. They also must be able to recognize the preferences of customers they have never met. It is a tall task, especially when you consider that many engineers—the people most charged with innovation—tend to have more technical skills than people skills.

Training and coaching can improve EQ in most people, and the net impact will be much greater. [I suggest that companies do more training and coaching—it comes and goes too quickly.]

Systems Thinking. H. L. Mencken once said that there is always a simple solution for every complex problem, but that will be wrong.

Systems thinking is a valuable piece of scaffolding. Not everyone understands what the unintended consequences of their own actions will be on other people and other departments. Training in systems thinking helps participants see the interconnectedness of different parts of a system. This creates an appreciation for others in the product-development web. Without the systems piece, partners can turn into accidental enemies, playing out roles that are antithetical to the good of the whole.

Systems thinkers look for patterns and structures beneath patterns, rather than just events. They look at the bigger picture to ascertain how they fit into that picture. Inventors look at more than their prized inventions—they see accounting systems, billing systems, and manufacturing challenges. In doing so, they avoid making mistakes and falling into organizational pits.

Like emotional intelligence, systems thinking can be taught. People can learn to use its fundamentals as a new language as they move forward in a product-development cycle. There will be fewer conflicts and turf wars.

Action-Learning Teams. People often learn better together. Teams approach, attack, and ponder challenging tasks together in what is sometimes referred to as *team learning.* Action learning is a refinement of this concept, focusing on complex challenges. In action learning, teams learn together by experimenting, coaching each other, and making mistakes. They do this methodically, and learn faster as they work together over a longer period of time. Action learning teams can overcome innovation challenges faster than can individuals.

In the context of innovation, action learning groups are able to provide a support system. The path to innovation is fraught with obstacles and loneliness; peer support helps with this. In addition, diversity contributes to successful innovation. Having differing viewpoints makes it easier to think "outside the box." Learning teams provide scaffolding for colleagues who are trying to come up with bold, new ideas.

Training in Innovation. Another form of scaffolding is to use specific training techniques targeted to thinking creatively. Company-wide training in brainstorming techniques, "blue ocean" techniques, and assumption-questioning techniques help to create a culture of innovation. Innovation is a process, and like other processes (billing, customer satisfaction, shipping), it can be taught and learned. Whirlpool and Cargill, for example, have company-wide training programs that train employees in innovation techniques. Cargill, in fact, has created a customized book to promote innovation in its company. Such programs open up eyes to possibilities and options for changing the status quo. It would be money well spent to train a few

87

employees in how to facilitate ideation sessions. They could be employed in a variety of departments in order to spark innovative thinking.

Moving an innovation effort forward requires scaffolding. Yes, it takes time, but with many key initiatives, it makes sense to go slow now in order to go faster later. Without scaffolding, creative innovators might end up feeling pressured or abandoned, hanging off window ledges. Their voices will not be heard and valuable initiatives will die on the vine without support systems. Or, worse yet, they will go to work for your competitors!

So, how do you become an innovative culture?

Changing an organization's culture is going to be a long and arduous process. There is no silver bullet, and the process itself will be fraught with obstacles. Some actions can help things move smoothly.

- *Make it a leadership priority.* Leaders must make innovation a priority for the organization. They need to talk about it, send out articles, hold ideation sessions, and provide resources for it.

  Change your attitude. Leaders have to adopt a positive attitude. Taking risks and making

---

(continued)

mistakes along the way are opportunities to learn, not things to be punished. This type of attitude must pervade management actions and communication.

- *Set up action-learning groups and roundtables.* Innovation takes high levels of collaboration. Leaders can mandate creation of such groups and provide training and coaching.

- *Begin scaffolding now.* Leadership should not waste time providing scaffolding for innovation. Training in creative-thinking techniques doesn't literally create innovation, but it provides the conditions where innovation can happen.

- *Gather and share resources.* Leaders need to make resources on innovation widely available and accessible. These do not have to be expensive: books, articles, training, or ideation sessions can have big impacts.

89

Take the Pulse of Your Organization: Culture

Evaluate your organization's culture by rating each question on a scale of 1 (hardly ever) to 5 (almost always). Calculate the average of your answers and rate your score.

_____ People in my organization learn from their failures.

_____ Management gives us space and time to be creative.

_____ People at all levels of the organization are involved in improvement schemes.

_____ Diversity of thought is encouraged at my organization.

_____ There are places at my organization for informal gatherings.

_____ My organization keeps a repository of ideas and products that have not yet been brought to the marketplace.

_____ My organization involves suppliers, customers, and other outsiders in new-product/service discussions.

_____ Designated people in my organization are always on the lookout for new trends in the industry.

(continued)

How to interpret your organization's score:

      1–2.5: Rigid and Life-Threatening
      2.5–4: Getting There...
      4.0–5: Innovation City!

Chapter 4:
Focus on the Customer

"We thought that we were selling the transportation of goods; in fact, we were selling peace of mind."

– Fred Smith, CEO
Federal Express,

If you take in a home game involving the St. Paul Saints, a minor league baseball team located in Minnesota, you will not be watching intently for two and a half hours as no-name players get hits or strike out. Instead, you will watch the mascot, a piglet, being chased around the infield. You might get a haircut in the stands or treat yourself to a chair massage, and you'll get to have lunch or dinner at one of the high-quality booths set up by local restaurants. Furthermore, you'll be able to enjoy the setting of the sun on a cool summer evening instead of sitting indoors like fans do at the major league game across town. The St. Paul Saints know that they are in the entertainment business, not the baseball business.

In the late 1990s, Whit Alexander and Richard Tait invented a board game. Their choices for marketing it were few. They could buy a booth at the New York City toy and game show, along with hundreds of other toy inventors, and hope that they get "discovered" and sell the game to Parker Brothers or Mattel. Or they could try to get the game into stores themselves (which would be a long, frustrating, and laborious process). Instead, they came up with a unique proposal. They showed the game to the CEO of Starbucks and suggested that the game's target market was the same as Starbucks's target market. Starbucks had never sold games, but the leadership saw potential. *Cranium's* inventors struck a deal to sell the game exclusively through Starbucks, and made sure that each Starbucks employee received a free copy of the game. *Cranium* and its spin-offs have turned out to be the best-selling games since *Pictionary*.

Understanding the Consumer

These two stories tell us much about marketing, getting close to the consumer, and the role of the consumer in innovation. You must always ask yourself three central questions:

- Who are your customers?
- What do they want?
- How can you reach them?

The process of innovation forces companies to understand the consumer, and it often takes consumers to help a company come up with something new.

The Basics

Marketing involves creating, selling, and distributing goods and services that the consumer wants and needs. Innovators need to understand consumer beliefs, attitudes, wants, and habits if they are to be successful. Consumers want products and services that "get a job done." Quality guru W. Edwards Deming and management guru Peter Drucker have both written extensively about the importance of understanding the consumer. Innovating requires deep understanding of the consumer's needs and then providing for those needs.

Innovators and marketers try to address consumers' needs and wants. Salsa has become popular in the last two decades in the United States, and dozens of options have appeared to satisfy everybody's taste buds. Visit the salsa aisle of a big-box grocery store, and dozens of options will pop out at you: mild, medium, hot, hotter, mango, pineapple, chili, and so on. Salsa comes in tall thin jars, round jars, short squat jars. The world probably does not need another salsa (except maybe a dark-chocolate salsa—*there's* an innovative idea!).

If you are going to develop a new product or service, you need to either totally delight the consumer, create a whole new category, or find a whole new group of customers. Doing any of these successfully means that you will have to do a lot of

95

creative thinking. Some questions that need to be addressed:

- Who is your customer? Who will your customer be in 10 years?

- Who is your competition ignoring?

- Where is innovation possible along the value chain?

- How can you maintain a favorable cost structure through your own production methods?

- How can you leverage your core competencies in new and different ways?

Asking these questions of members of your organization can mobilize them to think innovatively and differently about your product/service offerings. These open-ended questions are invitations to discuss, debate, and think creatively and originally.

Innovative organizations look for market segments that are underserved, and then develop creative new products and services that meet their needs. Distance learning programs were developed because someone realized that there were large numbers of people who wanted to further their education, but there were no nearby colleges. Early air conditioner units in China were loud and relatively ineffective, but were very inexpensive. Yet, for those who never had air conditioning, they were a blessing. The first suppliers understood this and made huge profits. Tata Automotive is introducing a car to the Indian market for $2,000, aimed mostly at consumers who have never had a car.

Another underserved segment in some parts of the world: affluent people who want more "bells and whistles" on normal products and are willing to pay for them. High-end restaurants with valet service, Blackberries with GPS systems, first-class airplane tickets, and minivans with built-in DVD players are all examples of successful market segmentation.

Find an underserved market segment—a group of potential consumers that other companies have left behind—and create offerings for them. You will have to try to identify unarticulated needs. I did not need an iPod, because I did not know there was a product that could do what it does. I would have never told a researcher that I wish there were cup holders on my baby's stroller, but they are there now, and I like them. Creative or innovative thinkers are always on the lookout for these unique opportunities that consumers themselves have not yet identified.

Beyond this hunt to develop products and services that will meet customer needs, innovators look for ways to partner with customers to create more-powerful offerings. Innovators need to harness the energy of their consumer "champions." Harley Davidson, the motorcycle manufacturer and distributor, is great at creating user groups; there

97

are Harley accessories and events for Harley enthusiasts. Heck, Harley lovers tattoo themselves with the logo and proudly wear gear covered with it. Have you ever seen someone with a Walgreens or Nordstrom's tattoo?

Ethnographic Observation and Research

If your goal is to develop and market products that consumers want, then you must find ways to get close to the customer. You need to get into the customer's head and find out how he or she thinks and makes consumption decisions.

A product design company was once approached by a food company that wanted to create new food-in-a-box products for large families. Teams of employees from both organizations visited the homes of large families and watched as mothers worked in the kitchen. They watched as the meals were prepared and observed moms interacting with their children. They noted how food was organized in the pantry and refrigerator. The team asked question after question, and acted just like anthropologists would in a Papua, New Guinea village: observing, asking, reflecting, and taking field notes. Their goal: to understand the deepest beliefs, attitudes, and desires of a typical mom trying to nutritionally and economically feed her family. The team used the data in ideation sessions, and were able to develop new product concepts for the client company.

Try This!

Observe consumers closely for an hour. Watch teens walking around a mall. Watch mothers in the cereal aisle of a grocery store. Observe people at a sporting event. Okay, now closely watch people drinking at a bar. What are their habits? What are their needs and wants? Be an anthropologist and try to understand them deeply.

The trick is to figure out what consumers want, need, and will buy. The method used in the example is sometimes referred to as ethnographic research, in which researchers observe *when and where* consumers are using the product or service. Researchers attempt, through observation and listening, to understand the deepest needs and desires of the consumers, because only when observing people in a natural setting can we find these inner mental and emotional churnings. The researchers involved in the large-family project concluded that parental self-esteem is the most important factor for the mothers: *Am I providing my family nutritious, healthy food? If I am, I am a good parent.*

A friend told me this story about Apple's attempts to get close to the consumer:

> *When we bought our first Mac in 1993 or 1994, we got a call from Apple asking if representatives of the company could come*

to our house and interview us. Rachel was gone, but I visited with them—they paid us $75 right on the spot! They took pictures of me at the computer (with Sophie, our dog, on my lap), asked questions about the color of the machines, what if it was a TV, what if it could play music, what if it were smaller, etc. This was years before iMac, iPod, iBook, and every other i-thing. I had no idea where the Apple folks were going with it until I started seeing computers that looked different. Clearly, Apple wouldn't have achieved any of those breakthroughs without investing in such field research.

When Marketing Research Does not Work

Marketing research may not always work. If you had surveyed customers in the 1980s as to whether or not they would buy a pet rock, the results would have been a resounding "no." Who would have wanted to spend $5 on a rock? But millions of people did so that Christmas.

If you had asked consumers in the late 1970s if they wanted to listen to a two-hour radio variety show centered on a boring, fictional town in northern Minnesota where all the men are strong, all the women good looking, and all the children are above average—and nothing ever

---

(continued)

> really happens—what would your response have been? Probably a strong "no," particularly on Saturday evening. Yet *Prairie Home Companion* is the most successful radio program in recent times.
>
> Consumers do not always know what they need and want. Innovators can tap into unarticulated needs by going against marketing research and conventional wisdom.

Observation is a powerful tool for understanding the consumer. The minivan with movable back seats was allegedly conceptualized when a car designer watched a couple struggle to put a sofa in the back of a minivan. Drivers holding hot cups of coffee between their legs led to the invention of cup holders in autos. Bored, disruptive children were what forced hospitals to provide toys and games in hospital waiting rooms. The key question is "Where do you see an unfulfilled need?"

Innovators use many other techniques that resemble ethnographic research. Several creative marketing researchers set up video cameras in stores to capture hundreds of hours of consumer behavior. Paco Underhill, author of the book *Why People Buy,* noticed that when aisles are too narrow and women get "butt brushed" by other shoppers, they usually leave the store immediately. Underhill says that people entering a store are in a "transition zone" and do not always notice signs and other messages. These insights help companies improve in-store design.

Trend Hunting

Innovative marketers hunt for trends that present marketing opportunities. There are many trend-hunting methods, formal and informal.

1. Read magazines, particularly outside of your field. Professionals from various disciplines look at the world differently. You should train yourself to spot a trend as it is emerging, and be able to look at the world from different perspectives.

2. Observe consumers in trendy places, such as Soho, Florence, London, Singapore.

3. Read blogs. Some blogs have large followings. What are these authors writing about, and what kind of responses do they get?

4. Follow different news sources from across the ideological spectrum. Catch reports on the BBC or Al Jazeera. Reputable sources will give you perspectives different from your own, and you might pick up on new trends.

5. Travel with your salespeople to visit their customers. Talk to your international counterparts.

What are they talking about? What is on their minds? What is the competition up to?

6. Look at what is around you with a wide angle lens. Often, innovations are on the periphery. A new competitor might come along from another industry. A novel kind of distribution system might work in your industry.

Resource
Made to Stick

Mike and Chip Heath, authors of the popular *Made to Stick*, published in 2007, suggest that it is not enough develop a product or service for a target market—organizations must communicate and sell the idea to the market. Heath and Heath set forth six factors for making ideas stick with consumers, which they call principles.

Principle 1: Simplicity
The product or service has to be understandable. Consumers will not spend lots of time trying to figure out a new concept.

Principle 2: Unexpectedness
Organizations must pique interest and curiosity of their target market. They must present some kind of "wow" factor.

(continued)

103

Principle 3: Concreteness
Ideas must be presented in tangible, sense-oriented language. Brains stick on concrete images, not fuzzy, abstract concepts.

Principle 4: Credibility
How do we make people believe our ideas and pitches? We must have facts or authorities behind our claims. In this era of fast information flow, consumers will make judgments as to whether or not they can believe us.

Principle 5: Emotions
How do we make people care about our ideas? We have to make them feel something. What can you say about your innovation that will make people feel deeply?

Principle 6: Stories
Mahatma Ghandi, Margaret Thatcher, Jesus, and many other great leaders used stories, not lectures, to convey their ideas. Why? Because stories touch the heart and the heart provokes action.

The Customer Process

Because of his wife's illness, a Maine farmer had to do the washing. He discovered how back-breaking the work was. He invented a mechanical washing machine. Car rental agencies perceived how frustrated customers were with the lengthy time it took to pick up a rental car; they streamlined the process. Chinese government officials watched blind people struggling to walk straight on sidewalks. They built lines of stone into sidewalks in major cities for the blind to follow.

Besides watching consumers in action, innovating thinkers map out their consumer processes and examine them step-by-step. Club Med, the all-inclusive resort chain, created worksheets for each of their consumer processes. These training sheets have three major sections:

1. The steps customers pass through.

2. The things that can go wrong at each step.

3. The systems that can be put in place to prevent those problems.

Let us say a Club Med guest wants to go wind surfing. The steps he or she would go through include: (1) Find the location; (2) Borrow a board; (3) Surf happily and safely; (4) Return the board.

105

What can circumvent a great experience? Sunburn? *Have sunscreen available.* Not finding the location? *Put up lots of informative signs.* Not know how to surf? *Offer training sessions.* Club Med is a high-end resort; it can command a high price because of its quality service. This system of anticipating problems and crafting systems to circumvent potential problems creates a superior customer experience.

Service providers have to be aware of "moments of truth"—those moments when a customer or potential customer comes into contact with the service provider. So, for a hospital, these moments of truth might be

- when scheduling an appointment;

- when registering;

- while waiting for a loved one to have surgery;

- while filling out endless, repetitive forms; or

- while waiting with small children to see a physician.

If you compare a hospital experience today to a similar experience thirty years ago, you would conclude that most United States hospitals have worked to minimize the pain in these moments of truth: Computer monitors inform you on the progress of your loved one in surgery. The waiting room has toys, activities, and internet connection, and free snacks. Most forms are computerized and are more easily managed. And furthermore, no fewer than five professionals confirm that it is indeed your *right* knee that needs surgery (they might even mark an X on that knee in magic marker).

Another way to look at the consumer experience is to think of the different stages of use of the product: purchase; transport to use area; setup; extras; maintenance; and disposal of the product. How could an organization be innovative in each of these dimensions? My mother recently wanted to buy a new television. We shopped at Best Buy because they will dispose of her aging television (it really belonged in a museum) for *free.* Free delivery? I will take it! Whatever will make my life easier! Printer cartridges at a discount? Count me in.

On a recent trip, I discovered a college with an interesting policy: If you buy a laptop through them, they will maintain it and give you access to their help desk. That is a huge benefit! So, it is not just about innovation in the product or service design; all the other steps of the consumption process are also important. More importantly, innovation can literally knock your competition out of the water.

The Value Chain

Where on the value chain can you innovate in order to create superior customer value? That question should haunt you. The value chain is the series of events between conception of the product or service and when it finally lands in the customer's hands or the customer disposes of it. WalMart and its largest supplier, Proctor and Gamble, saved money by moving from legal contracts to handshakes. WalMart created a cross-docking procedure that eliminated costs in their distribution system, thereby adding value. Most United States retailers put added value in their supply chains by sourcing from China and the Far East. As one company president said, "I can make it in China and ship it here for a third of the cost that I can make it here."

There are many ways to innovate in the value chain: Source raw materials that are cheaper, better, or easier to procure. Create new or refined internal processes. Cut costs and limit the time it takes to get the product to the end user. Add attributes to the product or service that will delight the customer, such as a maintenance package that puts the customer at ease. Innovative companies are constantly on the lookout for places to add value along the chain.

Pathways to the Consumer

1. Study the consumer. Be an anthropologist or a detective: observe, ask questions, take notes, examine the context. Listen carefully for needs that they have not yet articulated. What is missing from their lives? What do they want?

2. Look for trends. Find and scrutinize edgy Web sites. Research what is happening in Paris, Barcelona, Soho, or Shanghai if you cannot go there. Visit trendy spots in the U.S. as part of your research. Read magazines outside of your field, such as science and futurism magazines. Listen to people who are on the cutting edge via Web access (e.g., the Ted Conference lectures).

3. You and your competitors are satisfying customers' basic needs, but customers are also looking for extras. Think about things that would make your life easier.

4. Talk to your suppliers—they know what your competitors are doing. Probe them, because your competitors might know things about your customers that you do not.

5. Watch your competitors' market moves. Burger King allegedly watches where MacDonald's puts a new restaurant, and then locates a store down the block.

109

6. Watch for shifts in customer attitudes. Different generations have different attitudes toward life, work, technology, and recreation. If you do not follow those trends, you might lose your customer base.

7. Listen to customer feedback, particularly negative feedback. Customers who take time to complain care enough to help you become better.

8. Pay customers to be part of your ideation sessions. They can give insight that even your best people cannot provide.

Take the Pulse of Your Organization: Closeness to Consumers

Evaluate your organization by rating each question on a scale of 1 (hardly ever) to 5 (almost always). Calculate the average of your answers and rate your score.

_____ We regularly ask for customer feedback, and use that feedback.

_____ We bring customers into our innovation process.

_____ Our market researchers continually study our customers.

_____ All of our personnel have been trained in customer-service techniques.

_____ Our customers are able to communicate with us in a variety of ways.

_____ Our management regularly listens to customer panels.

_____ Our salespeople are constantly on the lookout for consumer trends.

How does your organization stack up?

1–2.5: Pathetic and Distant
2.5–4: Getting Closer
4.0–5: Cozy and Tight

111

Chapter 5:
The Process of Innovation

There is no single recipe for innovation. Some organizations look for a creative marketing or engineering guru to discover the "big idea" that will push the organization to new revenue heights. Others, such as a product development company in Minneapolis I'm familiar with use rigid, multi-step processes. Both approaches can work. In this chapter, we'll focus on several processes that organizations have used successfully.

New-Product Development

At the heart of the innovation process is new-product development. Most organizations have a delineated process for developing new products or services: identify the opportunity; generate the concept; evaluate the project; develop and test the product; and launch the product. Let's examine each of these.

1. **Identify the opportunity.**
   Where do new business ideas come from?

   Sales people. They have a good handle on what customers want.

Customers. They usually know what they need and what would make their lives easier.

Emerging markets. India and China have an emerging middle class with purchasing power.

Crises. 9/11 created an expanded market for security-related products and services.

Periphery markets. New inventions present other opportunities. For instance, cell phones create a huge market for software applications, ringtones, and leather cases.

Scientists. Geneticists are developing medical products to save lives, and exciting research in all fields of science will eventually lead to new products.

Technological breakthroughs. Stents, cell phones, GPS systems, pacemakers—need I say more?

Brainstorming sessions. Facilitated brainstorming with diverse participants can bring dozens of ideas.

Demographic changes. The Millennial generation that follows Generation X, born between 1977–1998, do not want the same services and products. Find out what makes them different. How can you woo this new group of consumers?

An innovative company constantly seeks opportunities to spark ideas that will lead to new revenue streams. Some ideas will not be right for today, but might be right five years from now. Some ideas will not work in their current form, but if they are tweaked, polished, or altered, they might be winners.

Simplest to Hardest

The late Charles Kettering, GM's head of research in 1912, nearly broke his arm trying to crank-start his car one morning. A few days later, a friend was killed while crank-starting his car. Kettering sat down and listed 10 major obstacles to overcome before cars could be started automatically. He arranged them from simplest to hardest, and started to solve the problems one at a time. The result was his first invention: the Delco self-starter, considered to be the world's second most important automobile invention. (Take note of the process Kettering used.)

---

2. Generate the concept.

Ideas are raw; they must be formed, molded, and articulated. Concepts have to be stated in terms of customer needs. A concept for a new food product might be "a nutritious, easy-to-make breakfast drink aimed at the teen market." A concept for a new kind of healthcare

115

delivery might become "a fast, no-appointment-needed, inexpensive health care clinic aimed at people with common, minor illnesses and ailments."

Ideas come from many sources, but it is usually a team of production, R and D, and marketing people who hammer out a concept statement that will be articulate and understandable to many different internal stakeholders. The concept statement has to be specific enough to give direction to the product developer, and general enough to allow for wiggle room.

3. **Evaluate the product.**
At this point, the entire product is evaluated for organizational mission fit, financial viability, marketability, resource availability, and technological feasibility. Sometimes this is called a *concept screen,* because the concept is screened through several filters. Questions like these are asked during this phase:

1) Will this project be profitable?

2) What is the projected ROI?

3) Is mass production feasible?

4) Can we obtain the necessary raw materials?

5) Does this project fit with the organizational mission? Strategic priorities?

6) Does the target market want this product? How much will people pay for it?

There are several possible results of the evaluation process. The concept can be sent back to committee for further refinement, or tabled because of competing priorities. It might be killed because the return on investment is too small, or could be sent on to product development.

4. Develop and test the product.

A cross-functional product-development team should include people from production, marketing, research and development, packaging engineering (if needed), and accounting. The team develops timelines and work plans and sketches out a marketing plan. Raw material suppliers are then sourced.

Most importantly, product-development teams develop prototypes. Several gallons of a new cleaning compound might be mixed in a vat and then tested at customer locations. A CAD/CAM rendition of a new car might be presented to prospective customers. Models might be created out of clay or cardboard. These prototypes are usually malleable enough to be altered as needed.

At any point along the way (or at every step), a "Go/No go" decision needs to be made. If the product falls short on any criteria, the

117

product might be killed. If it is still a "Go" at this point, it might be placed in a test market—that is, introduced into several markets in order to monitor how it does. One downside of test marketing is that the company tips its hand to the competitor. On the other hand, a competitor might try to sabotage the test marketing by buying up the experimental product or flooding the market with their own coupons.

5. **Launch the product.**
   The product or service, if it has gotten this far, now needs to be introduced to the marketplace. The launch stage is usually very frenetic, as there are a multitude of last-minute details. Can you imagine the logistics of getting a new product into warehouses all over the country or the world? Promotions, advertising, packaging, and internal and external messages all need to be coordinated. Salespeople need to be trained and motivated. Manufacturing needs to churn out the product without a hitch. If the manufacturing is done in Asia, the product needs to be built and shipped. Sometimes companies do phased rollouts, introducing the new product to different regions sequentially rather than simultaneously.

Fast Prototyping

Companies are always looking for ways to stream-
line the product-development process. For
instance, in the past, it often took five years for an
automaker to take a design and turn it into a new
car on the showroom floor. Market needs might
have changed in that time, but a faster competitor
might even beat you to the market while you do
your market analysis. In fact, you are not likely to
have a few years to wait for the income stream
from this new product. Some companies, therefore,
are turning to fast prototyping as a solution to this
innovation dilemma.

A few years back, I worked with a group of
Asian military personnel facing an interesting
problem. The time it took to test the hydraulics of
their Chinook helicopters before they could be sent
out on a mission was 3.5 hours, far too long for war
time conditions. Our innovation group was told to
reduce that turnaround time significantly. First, we
observed the actual situation—the hydraulics being
tested. Next, we sent several teams out to study the
dynamics of the hydraulics and other hydraulic systems. One group searched the Internet for solutions, while another went out to the local port and
watched how the hydraulic systems of large loading
cranes were tested. A third group visited an eleva-
tor manufacturer to learn how it tested hydraulic
systems. The groups came back and synthesized

119

their data, and we created a new concept for testing the helicopters' systems. It took our final conceptual prototype 30 minutes to test the hydraulics of the Chinook. Mission accomplished through fast prototyping.

Fast prototyping involves some of the same steps as new-product development. Yet, these are done faster, often with an outside "ideation" company.

Five Steps to Fast Prototyping

In a fast prototyping process:

1. *Schedule observations.* Observe the consumers in their real situations while they are consuming or using products. Take copious field notes, listen well and, when possible, ask questions.

2. *Review and analyze the data.* In the best situation, several teams or several individuals have captured data from a variety of locations. These individuals and teams converge to display, sift through, analyze, reconfigure, and attempt to deeply understand the data.

3. *Hold a brainstorming session.* The team brainstorms possible solutions. At this stage, flipchart paper is flying as many ideas are

---

(continued)

120

Five Steps to Fast Prototyping (concluded)

---

generated (without judgment). A trained facilitator uses divergent thinking techniques with the team to produce as many ideas as possible.

4. *Fast prototyping.* At this stage, the team uses convergent thinking techniques to develop possible prototypes. Groups can use paper, cardboard, paper clips, pipe cleaners, play-dough, clay, Legos, and other modeling material to create prototypes. The point is not to get it exactly right, but to create working models to discuss and refine later.

5. *Evaluate and tweak.* Most organizations have evaluation criteria for new products and services. After a prototype is built, it can be presented to a larger group of stakeholders for tweaking and evaluation.

These steps apply to products and processes.

Many permutations exist for each of these steps. I once did some consulting work with infantry soldiers in an Asian country. We were charged with finding ways to reduce the number of night-vision goggles that were lost by soldiers. We watched videos of soldiers placing the goggles on their helmets. This was a cumbersome five-minute process, involving the use of plastic ties. Our client did not

121

tell us about the plastic ties; it took observing the process. We ended up creating an efficient clipping system that took only 5–10 seconds. The clip process worked, but deviations from the process also worked, and in fact turned out to be better.

Other Innovation Techniques

The beauty of innovation is that many techniques will help you elicit and organize ideas, such as challenging; flowcharts; creative problem solving; attribute lists; and "Blue Ocean" innovation. Some of the techniques and processes are organized forms of brainstorming that enable groups to look at problems and opportunities in new ways.

Challenging

In the higher education industry thirty years ago, the industry norms were:

- Students came to campus.

- Most students were in their late teens and early twenties.

- Professors were content experts.

- Classes were conducted during the week.

- Professors lectured content that only a few people were privy to, and students took notes.

- Most students were white and American-born.

Look at what has happened in recent decades. Online education programs allow 68-year-old students from East Podunk to earn undergraduate or graduate degrees. Students can access the same content as professors on the Internet. The professor transforms from the "expert" with all the information to the "connector" of information and knowledge. Students from different generations and continents can get an education anywhere and anytime. Industry assumptions have been successfully challenged.

Innovation begins by challenging or questioning the status quo, using a statement such as:

The world can be better with a _____.

We can challenge or question the world, a product line, or an existing group of products as they are. A manager might have a group of employees challenge all of the industry norms, asking: What are those things that all members of this industry take for granted? What beliefs are true no matter what? What are the stable drivers of the industry, or the foundations that make the industry tick? The next big industry innovations might come out of such "challenges."

You can do the same thing on a smaller scale. Have a group list all of their assumptions about a product or a business problem, and then systematically challenge those assumptions. Then ask

123

them to reverse those assumptions, posing questions such as: *What if the opposite were true?* These challenges pry open assumptions to shine a light on other possibilities that might lead to significant innovations.

Resource
The Art of Innovation
by Tom Kelley

This book shows how the product design firm Ideo designs new products. The book details how Ideo does a "deep dive" into the customers' needs and technology possibilities in order to create new designs. This book gives the reader a glimpse behind the magical curtain of product creation.

Flowcharts

Flowcharting is not new, but it has been popularized by the quality movements. Flowcharting lists sequential steps of a process, and divides them into decisions or actions. A team can then scrutinize each of the steps and question the necessity of each by asking:

- What steps do our employees go through to get a piece of work done?

- Do we need this step?

- Can the task be performed in another more efficient way?

If a manager asks a group to try to create a new version of an existing process, some individuals will be overwhelmed by its complexity. By breaking the process down into its component parts, each step becomes more manageable and understandable, and will ultimately be improved.

Customer-focused flowcharts

Traditional flowcharting focuses on the process from the viewpoint of the organization. You can reverse this to list the steps that a customer goes through to use a product or service. For instance, to enjoy a dinner out at a restaurant, I must identify the restaurant, find it, park, be seated, identify an excellent menu item, and order. After I am served (in a timely fashion), I eat, accept the bill, pay the bill, and leave.

At each step in this process, what can go wrong? In a customer-focused flowchart process, a restaurant owner considers, at each step, how to make this experience a delightful one. How about a valet service for parking, or a waiting area with a fish tank and coloring books and crayons to delight my children? How about free hors d'oeuvres if I have to wait more than 15 minutes?

125

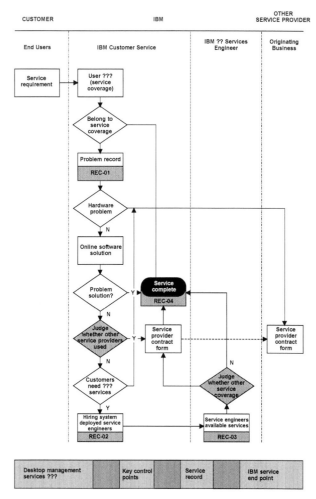

Source: http://www.edrawsoft.com/images/examples/
Services%20Flowchar_full.png

The three steps of customer-focused flowcharting are fairly clear, answering in turn each of these questions:

- What steps do our customers or clients go through when using our product or service?

- At each step, what can go wrong?

- At each of these steps, what can we do to ensure customer delight?

Improvement may require minor tweaks or major innovations. (You will never know which until you brainstorm for solutions.)

A variation of this approach is to use a template of the customer process in order to look for innovations. The template typically covers these areas:

- Selection
- Order process
- Delivery
- Learning How to Use
- Use
- Reorder
- Maintenance
- Disposal

Now, how can a company delight its customers in each of these areas? How can a template make each of these steps seamless, easy, effortless, uncomplicated, uplifting, delightful, amazing, and exciting? Successful companies map this out meticulously.

127

A friend experienced this type of customer-centric service at Disneyworld several years ago:

After spending a few days in one of the Disney resorts in Orlando, I received a phone message: I had left a pair of cheap shorts behind in the hotel room. Did I want them to send the shorts? Of course, this was not just a lost-and-found call, but a marketing connection—they reminded me that I visited Disney World, asked me how I enjoyed my trip, and let me know that they wanted me to return.

Try This!

Have a team at your organization create a customer-centric flowchart. Choose a process that a customer proceeds through. Ask these questions as you create the steps on a big piece of paper:

- What steps do our customers or clients go through when using our product or service?

- At each step, what can go wrong?

- At each of these steps, what can we do to ensure customer delight?

Post this chart on a bulletin board for all to see. Perhaps it will encourage others to do the same.

Creative Problem Solving

The Creative Problem Solving Institute formulated a process almost a half century ago, and has tinkered with it ever since. The basic stages/steps are:

1. *Objective finding.* What is the real objective of this problem-solving search?

2. *Fact finding.* What do we know, and what do we not know about this situation? What else would be nice to know?

3. *Problem/challenge finding.* Given the objective and what we know, what is the real challenge here?

4. *Idea finding.* In what ways might we do this? This is the divergent, brainstorming part of the process.

5. *Solution finding.* In this convergent step, what are the best ideas of the bunch?

6. *Acceptance finding.* How can we get acceptance through management, customers, salespeople, and other stakeholders?

The steps can be worked through quickly or for hours at a retreat. Notice that like all good innovation processes, the steps include both convergent and divergent thinking.

129

Created equally?

Are all innovations created equally? No, not really. Let's look at several kinds.

Industry changers. The car, the laptop computer, the iPod, Amazon.com—these innovations were so uniquely new, they changed everything.

Radical innovation. These innovative concepts become industry "leaders." Barnes and Noble changed what we thought about bookstores. Hybrid cars changed how we think about energy consumption.

Major process innovations. Universities have replaced the time-consuming registration lines with online registration. Supermarkets and other stores allow self-checkout.

Incremental improvements. Often made in connection with Six Sigma or Lean Manufacturing, these quality and productivity measures can cut millions of dollars in costs.

Attribute listing. Another innovation technique is to list the parts of a product, and then brainstorm how you might improve on each part. For instance, if I want to redesign a high chair, the component parts include legs, back, height, eating surface, latching mechanism, and seat. My team and I would examine and look at options for each part. The options for the legs might be to use steel, aluminum, or wood; put it on rollers; make it collapsible; paint it; add decorations; make it adjustable; and/or add cup holders. To create a better high chair, we would consider all the options for component parts. Some could be mixed or matched, and others could be new concepts.

"Blue ocean" innovation. According to the authors of the best seller *Blue Ocean Strategies*, companies have two competition options: They can compete in red oceans, where competitors are tearing out each others' flesh and creating blood pools in the ocean, or compete in blue oceans, where there is no competition. The key to finding the blue ocean is to ask and answer four questions:

1. Which factors that the industry takes for granted should be eliminated?

2. Which factors should be reduced well below the industry standard?

3. Which factors should be raised well above the industry standard?

4. Which factors that the industry has never offered should be created?

The authors of *Blue Ocean Strategies* suggest that successful organizations use these questions continually in order to find "blue ocean" space for new products. In the Twin Cities, where I live, we have an extremely competitive grocery store industry, with many players trying to gain an edge. If I were trying to create a new kind of grocery store, answering these questions would clarify some options. Reduce the number of offerings? Aldi does. Eliminate bags? Aldi does. Create new offerings, such as adding an optical shop, a deli, a photo shop, or a coffee shop? How about a post office? (Byerly's Food Stores has one.) Reduce customer service? (Cub Foods does to cut costs.) Each of these players in the Twin Cities' grocery industry carves out their market niches by using these questions.

Resource
Joel Barker's *Tactics of Innovation*

Futurist Joel Barker developed a checklist of attributes that an innovation will need if it is to catch on. He produced a DVD called "Tactics of Innovation," that gives excellent examples for each of the tactics and can prevent individuals and organizations from making mistakes when introducing innovations into the marketplace.

Tactic 1: *Upside, yes* (Is there a perceived advantage to the user?)

Tactic 2: *Downside, no* (Will the consequences minimal if it fails?)

(continued)

Tactic 3:	*Seemingly simple* (Is it easy for the user to understand?)
Tactic 4:	*Small steps* (Is the change implemented using small increments?)
Tactic 5:	*Clear message* (Is the language clear to the user?)
Tactic 6:	*Compatible fit* (Will it feel familiar to what the user currently experiences?)
Tactic 7:	*Credible messenger* (Is the presenter believable and credible to the user?)
Tactic 8:	*Reliable performance* (Does it work, without breaking down?)
Tactic 9:	*Easy in* (How easy is it for the user to try it?)
Tactic 10:	*Easy out* (How easy is it for the user to get out?)

(See the Bibliography for more information on the video.)

The Process, Summarized

Many roads lead to innovation. The beginning is clear: destroy, unlearn, dismantle. Unless you are willing to let go of the existing processes, products, or ways of doing things, you cannot move ahead into new territory.

The next step is idea generation: listening to suppliers, holding brainstorming sessions, letting scientists tinker with ideas, looking at adverse conditions that might suggest a need, etc. You need acute observers: people listening, observing, connecting, and taking good notes.

After an idea is generated, the innovation process becomes more focused. How can we make this work? How can we make this profitable? How can we get people to buy this product? Can our operations make this product or service? Can we undercut the competition, or destroy them with our bells and whistles? How can we ensure success? Or is it low-risk enough that we can just slap it out there and see if it works?

At this point, teams of people from different functional areas of the organization will have to come together to move the idea forward and introduce the innovation into the marketplace. This step generally requires paying attention to a myriad of details.

Key Points

- Most companies have a pretty clear set of stages for introducing new products into the marketplace: idea identification; concept generation; project evaluation; product development; and launch.

- Most organizations do not employ an organized process to develop and bring to fruition new ideas, but there are many quick ways to do fast prototyping and ideation.

- Management needs a way to develop and capture new ideas, so that the organization always has a few in the pipeline.

- The process of innovation contains divergent aspects (developing many new ideas) and convergent aspects (deciding which are worthwhile).

Take the Pulse of Your Organization:
How effective are *your* innovation practices?

Evaluate your organization by rating each question on a scale of 1 (hardly ever) to 5 (almost always). Calculate the average of your answers and rate your score.

_____ Everyone in my organization understands the new-product-development cycle and executes it well.

_____ Everyone in my organization is encouraged to develop ideas through formal brainstorming sessions.

_____ My organization has an organized system for developing and capturing new ideas.

_____ My organization has processes in place to reduce the time it takes to bring new products and services into the marketplace.

_____ Most employees here feel free to question assumptions about how we do business.

_____ Innovation is the job of all employees. We have in-place processes to get everyone to think creatively, rather than just rely on a couple of scientists or product developers.

How does your organization rate?

      1–2.5: Innovation...WHAT?
      2.5–4: Getting there...
      4.0–5: We have a well-oiled machine

Chapter 6:
Creative Collaboration

"Why creative collaboration? Why now? Many employees of organizations—private, public, or non-profit—are asked to do more with less. Budgets are cut but the work remains. We have to figure out how to work better and faster with the resources which are left—that means you and me. The key to success in the coming decades is collaborating creatively and efficiently. Two plus two needs to equal 34, not three."

– Richard Brynteson

Despite the stereotypical "lone innovator/inventor," most innovations move forward because of the efforts of teams of people. Generally, cross-functional teams push inventions out the corporate door into the marketplace. Groups of researchers combine their findings into viable designs. Customers and product developers team up to create better, more useful products. Even Michelangelo had 13 artists working for him on the ceiling of the Sistine Chapel. Interesting ideas emerge from eureka moments, but it takes groups to introduce them into the marketplace.

Systems Approach

Like it or not, we are all part of several larger systems, so if we want to innovate, we will have to work within these larger systems. This larger system includes customers, suppliers, partners, and competitors. Unless we see ourselves as part of that ecology within our industry, we might miss vital pieces of the business puzzle.

Relationships with Suppliers

Creativity and innovation cause ripples in supply chains. Can your suppliers provide the right raw material? Here is an example of what I mean: I have to hire adjunct instructors to teach business courses at the university where I teach. If I create an innovative, outside-the-box curriculum that will dazzle and excite students, I need to make sure that others can teach it. There have been times when I have produced new types of course content, only to have my adjunct professors throw it out and go back to the old way of teaching it.

Relationships with Customers

Harnessing the ideas of your customers is an art, but a worthy one. Customers can be great innovation partners and they are eager to tell you what they think. Listen! Use traditional marketing-research mechanisms such as focus groups, surveys, interviews, and observation. Creative ethnography is also helpful (as discussed earlier). Consider bringing customers to your meetings at the headquarters, and make them part of your teams. In doing so, you could be turning your consumers into producer-consumers.

Resource
No More Teams
by Michael Schrage

Schrage's seminal book outlines techniques and dynamics for creative collaboration. Schrage looks in depth at how to make creative collaboration happen in organizations using white space, diversity, and other organizational dynamics. He elaborates on the prototyping process and explores how it can be used effectively.

Relationships with Competitors

Welcome to the brave new world: an open marketplace of ideas, innovations, and inventions. The solid line between competitors is not as obvious as it used to be. The vicious competitor of the past might now be the current collaborator or vital member of your supply chain. Perhaps you do not yet have the resources for an innovative new research project, or the scope of the project you are planning is much too large for one organization.

Creative collaboration might make sense in these circumstances. The financial institutions in the United States have been faltering and teetering toward bankruptcy; now is a great time for them to collaborate on solutions.

Open-Source Partners

Who really has the keys to brilliance, creative break-throughs, or the hearts and minds of customers? Ultimately, an organization does not really know where its next innovation is coming from. With open sourcing, partners emerge from nooks and crannies that were never envisioned by groups of 50-year-old execs in board rooms. That is why organizations must stay open to partnership possibilities, and be ready to create new opportunities as they emerge. "We have never done that before" is no longer a valid reason in these turbulent times. Certainly, no one organization has all of the world's intellectual capital for new innovations.

As the artificial barriers of competitor, supplier, customer, insider and outsider erode, new forms of communication will be needed to encourage collaboration between these agents. Collaborative software enables partners in Bangalore, Brittany, Belfast, and Biloxi to work together fluidly. Social networking sites such as Facebook, Twitter, and MySpace make instant and continual communication the norm. Other mechanisms, such as conference calling, video conferencing, and Skype create opportunities for virtual communication. All of these innovations make creative collaboration more accessible.

Techniques for Creative Collaboration

Innovations often emerge from creative collaboration. People work together creatively to produce something new and different, using an array of new techniques for creative collaboration.

Access to Information for Collaboration

It is important to have places where ideas are collected, combined, and grow into useful innovations. Blogs, computerized discussion boards, flipcharts, white boards, and idea-capturing software are all places to post and make accessible information that will be useful to people who are collaborating creatively. First-shift nurses use logs to communicate patient information to second-shift nurses. On blogs or discussion boards, participants can build on each other's ideas asynchronously, long after a brainstorming meeting, where flipchart paper flies and ideas and action plans are captured.

These communication "spaces" matter because they are neutral places for captured ideas. The ideas

141

are no longer Richard's or Jill's; they belong to the white space. Ego is more easily pushed aside, so real communication can happen.

Creative Abrasion

Innovation creates excitement and exuberance, and it happens at the confluence of ideas. When participants are brainstorming, some ideas will inevitably run counter to other ones. Innovation is not always pretty. Sparks and fur will fly, and ideas will bounce wildly and boomerang back. People will step on each other's toes. Well-meaning "abrasion" may occur; creative abrasion should be encouraged. Polite, well-mannered people sitting at a table with hands folded and mouths shut rarely invent anything. Active, vociferous, wild-minded people *do,* but they can come across as abrasive.

Diversity

Diversity breeds innovation. What you do not want are people who think the same way. Diversity comes in many forms: gender, age, functional roles, religion, race, thinking styles, information-processing patterns, and so on. Diverse points of view allow for different angles of vision and differing patterns of perspective.

Meeting Places

Creative collaboration can only take place where people can come together. Informal places such as a break room will work, as will formal "innovation" rooms (I see more and more of them). I believe that cubicles produce more-creative collaboration than offices: there are no doors to close, so people are more comfortable walking into another person's cube than walking into someone's office at the spur of the moment. Informal discussions, under these circumstances, are encouraged by this setup.

Action-Learning Groups

One powerful way to spur innovation is to set up action-learning groups where people get together on a regular basis to learn and grow together while they work on innovative practices. They learn innovative techniques and help one another use them effectively. Each meeting can focus on one or more innovation projects, using and keeping track of best practices. Members of the group hold one another accountable for meeting goals and deadlines.

Action learning teams not only create new ideas, they keep old ideas alive and find new uses for them. They make sure that ideas have a shot at becoming real products by making sure that they are moving through a new-product pipeline. Action-learning groups also give an ear to others with ideas and projects in mind.

143

Groups wanting to encourage innovation should train and keep these action-learning teams together. Tactics of innovation need to be taught so they will become a regular part of the organization's culture. Training in group cohesion and innovative techniques is often necessary. Many employees are lone wolves who are accustomed to working by themselves on projects, and therefore might need guidance in how to work efficiently and effectively with others.

Communities of Practice

Communities of practice are groups with a common interest or domain who engage in the process of collective learning, like a tribe learning to survive. Communities of practice are broader than action-learning groups. In fact, an action-learning group is often part of a community of practice. Communities of practice exist inside and outside of organizations. They share resources: tools, stories, shared practices, and ways of addressing reoccurring problems. They are involved in individual and collective learning and growing.

The concept of communities of practice is not new. The Transcendentalist movement used them; Emerson, Thoreau, Alcott, and others met formally and informally in Boston in the 1800s and talked philosophy. The Impressionist painters in Paris met in cafes and talked technique. Many ministers and priests meet weekly with colleagues in the same community to talk about readings for the week and other matters. Groups of therapists meet and talk about their most-difficult cases and various treatment options.

A community of practice can help an organization be more innovative. Innovation circles, groups, contests, projects, seminars, and displays are visible activities where people can talk about their initiatives and projects. When groups share best and worst practices and keep the creative juices flowing, innovation will move forward faster.

Examples of Creative Collaboration

Creative collaboration is the best path toward innovation. Together, we are smarter, more creative, and more resourceful than we are individually. Here are some examples of creative collaboration:

Ideo. The "deep dive" process used by the design company Ideo is a good example of creative collaboration. The company's diverse group of product designers works on problems and opportunities using a series of steps similar to the ones spelled out in the "Fast Prototyping" section of this book. Their playful office space is filled with materials and mechanisms that can be used to design the next great invention. Designers diverge and converge to redesign products, such as a better shopping cart.

They are having fun while they explore and innovate.

General Electric. General Electric is famous for its leadership development center in Crotonville, New York. The Company schedules "workouts," where managers take each other on over policies and procedures. Many of GE's creative think tanks grew out of such sessions.

Edison's Menlo Park. One of the first great invention think tanks in American history was created by Thomas Edison at Menlo Park. At any given time, he had five to fifteen engineers working there, side by side. At close proximity, they could interact and build on each other's ideas. Edison's think tank produced more than 400 patents, including the telegraph and telephone.

Disney Studios. Walt Disney and his brother kept hundreds of creative minds busy in the early days of the Disney Company. Many Disney people worked side by side on cinematographic innovations; 750 people created *Snow White and the Seven Dwarfs*, at that time the most innovative movie ever made. Some referred to that project as "a dream with a deadline."

Habitat for Humanity. The organization Habitat for Humanity, backed by former United States President Jimmy Carter, has been one of the most successful collaborations in history. This organization builds houses for needy families across the globe. To build a single house, the organization pulls together a multitude of volunteers, funders, building professionals, and government officials. Corporations sometimes use a Habitat for Humanity building project for team building among its staff. Habitat for Humanity has built and provided thousands of homes for families over the past couple of decades.

Books for Africa. Books for Africa collects, sorts, ships, and distributes books to children in Africa. This organization has shipped 21,000,000 books to Africa in the past 20 years. Its success has been a result of collaborations between shipping companies, Somalia youths, OPEC, large United States corporations, small Nigerian states, community service "volunteers," and thousands of book donors.

Key Points

- Collaboration is extremely important to the innovation process. Lone innovators are a rare species.

- Collaboration can be learned. Employees can be taught techniques and learn how to work with others during the creative process.

- Action-learning groups can accomplish much together as they fine-tune their ability to collaborate.

- Diversity, idea sharing, and creative abrasion are all essential for effective creative collaboration.

Take the Pulse of Your Organization: Creative Collaboration

Evaluate your organization by rating each question on a scale of 1 (hardly ever) to 5 (almost always). Calculate the average of your answers and rate your score.

_____ I enjoy attending task force meetings.

_____ I get a rush from all we accomplish in a short amount of time.

_____ We appreciate differences in individuals even when those differences annoy us.

_____ Informal brainstorming and meetings are encouraged.

_____ Everyone understands the processes that it takes to get work done.

_____ People feel free and willing to build on one another's ideas.

_____ We hire people with many different perspectives in our organization.

How does your organization rate?

1–2.5: We rarely speak the same language
2.5–4: We can move toward agreement
4.0–5: We read each others' minds

Chapter 7:
Innovation: The Future

Predicting the future of innovation is like predicting the future itself—it is difficult and fraught with all sorts of variables and unexpected events that carry far-reaching consequences: 9/11, Hurricane Katrina, the faltering of the banking system, the bankruptcy of Iceland, and so on. Some trends, however, seem to be in place.

Smaller. Nanotechnology advances will produce small-scale innovations. Entire newspapers might soon be printed on sheets of plastic, only to be replaced with the next day's varieties. Some day, a small portable chip will carry all of our medical information.

Biomedical breakthroughs. The medical products industry will produce more devices and medications geared to prolonging and improving life.

Green. Environmental degradation and resource scarcity will require occupants of the planet to be more efficient in using resources. Demand and incentives such as tax breaks will bring about a flowering of green products and processes.

Partnerships. Better and better communication technology will blur the lines between supplier, company, and customer. Consumers and suppliers will take on cocreation roles in supply-chain innovations.

24/7 Connectivity. Faster and faster tools for communication and social networking will become available as the Millennial generation, dragging the other generations with it, will insist on 24/7 connectivity. The backlash from this—people becoming less savvy about face-to-face communication—will spawn another soft-skills industry, bent on helping with old-fashioned communication.

Retro. In a backlash against an individualistic, fast-paced, virtual communication-based society, people will be more attracted to community-based living projects. Participants will share resources, from cars to bikes to lawn mowers and even physical space. Residents in these collective living situations will learn to live together and leave a smaller carbon footprint on the planet.

Getting Started: Basic Techniques

So, where does innovation start? Some people think that to be innovative, one has to start big. Often it is best to start small and get some successes under the belt before growing the initiatives. Here are some techniques that can be used as beginner steps:

Brainstorming sessions. Brainstorming or ideation sessions are very useful because they generate many ideas from many sources. In these sessions, people can collect, organize, and work with many ideas, including ideas with divergent and convergent parts. Wild ideas are encouraged, and nothing is criticized or thrown out. Organizations can use such sessions to:

- Select partners for new ventures.
- Find high potential.
- New arenas and markets
- Create easier, cheaper, better, and more convenient products or services.
- Find ways to use organizational resources in interesting new combinations.

Quick prototyping. Quick prototyping is just that: get a prototype out there for others to react to. Groups can do this all at once or in smaller increments.

Innovation room. If the resources are available (mostly space and materials), consider creating a dedicated innovation room. It sends a message to

153

the organization that *innovation is important.* The room should be equipped with flipchart paper, white boards, computers, and other tools for information collection and sharing. It should also have materials to create prototypes: pipe cleaners, straws, foam, clay, Playdough, knickknacks, Legos, magic markers, and so on. There should be movable furniture in order to encourage flexibility in activities.

Anthropologist teams. Innovation often requires that people get out of the office. Teams should go out and observe customers consuming your product/service or your competitor's product/service. Watch customers from a target market that you wish to serve. What do they need or want? What job do they need done? Have a diverse group of observers and tell them to take notes. Then, discuss those notes in feedback and ideation session.

Creativity techniques. Creativity techniques can loosen up the thinking of a group. A few simple ones are:

- List as many uses of a brick or paperclip as you can in five or ten minutes.

- List all the attributes of an item (say, a baby stroller) and see how many permutations of each you can think of. Then, collect and combine them.

- Ask 25 questions about a tree or orchid.

New areas and markets. Ask probing market related questions:

- Where is the industry going? Is there a different, lucrative direction?

- Is there an underserved, or completely unserved, market segment out there?

- Is there a product or service offering you can offer for the "frugal consumer" that is new and different?

- What product/service improvements are consumers willing to pay for?

Book or video groups. Start a book group in your organization. Use one of the books or videos referred to in this book to start the discussion. Always bring the discussion back to how these techniques can be of use to your organization.

Work process. Have a group focus on one of your work processes. At every step, have participants ask "Why do we need this step?"

Study behavioral science. New research in behavioral patterns such as smoking, obesity, exercise, reading, and computer usage can give you clues on trends and ideas for new products or services.

A Scenario

Global warming is in the news constantly. While the causes are hotly debated, the results are becoming painfully clear, and the people of planet earth need to start remedying this situation. Innovative thinking is what is needed for solutions.

We need to find new, renewable energy sources. Some are already proving to be less expensive and more efficient (e.g., wind power).

Conservation strategies should be improved and promoted more aggressively. One conservation strategy is to impose carbon taxing on individuals (taxes and tax incentives).

Opportunities exist to invent new electronic gadgets that will show the user how much energy is needed to power and run a device. If a device told me how much a ten-minute hot shower costs versus a three-minute shower, for example, I would be able to make an educated choice.

It is important that we change attitudes, however. Communities of practice can help to promote using less energy and create community momentum and spirit around reducing our carbon footprint.

The Manhattan project in the 1940s and the NASA moon initiative in the 1960s provided a goal and a sense of urgency that innovators could rally around. Reducing global warming should be another one of these initiatives invested with a sense of urgency.

Chapter 8:
Conclusion

Thomas Edison was the epitome of the American innovator. He had 1,093 patents in his lifetime and was responsible for inventions that improved the lives of millions of Americans. He was involved in the invention of the phonograph, the light bulb, the motion picture camera, electricity-producing plants and many other inventions.

Edison's life as an inventor illustrates many important points about what it takes to be successful at innovation.

His career was an accident. He was selling gum and candy. One day, he saved a three-year-old child from a runaway train. The child's grateful father hired Edison to work in a telegraph office.

Attention to detail. Edison worked out the nitty gritty details of his inventions himself, and was always experimenting with new materials to see how they performed (he even strung his own telegraph wire.)

Creative collaboration. Thomas Edison collaborated with hundreds of people. He understood that he possessed only part of the skills and knowledge to accomplish his goals., and that he would need the expertise, financing, and connections of others.

Emotional intelligence. Edison had strong interpersonal and self-awareness skills. He was able to mobilize hundreds of people to work with him and follow his vision. He removed his own self-imposed constraints and believed in what seemed impossible, and he convinced others to share his belief.

A strong and articulated vision. In 1879, Edison said, "We will make electricity so cheap that only the rich will burn candles." His vision of cheap, affordable electricity became a reality.

Self-improvement. Certainly, Edison is among the most brilliant Americans in our history. His favorite pastimes were reported to be reading and experimenting. With his restless mind, Edison was always looking into new concepts and new ideas for inventions and innovations.

Resilience. Edison was penniless in 1869, and almost went bankrupt several times, but he always bounced back. When his plant burned down in West Orange, New Jersey, he rebuilt it immediately, bigger and better. When he lost an important source of raw material because of World War I, he figured out how to synthesize it.

Customer focus. Edison saw how the common person struggled in his/her day-to-day life. His innovations constantly created better lives for people in communication, utilities, entertainment, and other important arenas.

Public/private partnerships. Edison worked with the United States government on many innovations. During World War I, he invented many products and systems for the war effort. His straddling of the public/private line became the model for many inventors who came after him.

Systems thinking. Edison had a keen sense how things fit together and affected each other. He realized that his light bulbs were useless without a power source, so he invented one.

Institutionalized collaboration. Perhaps Edison's greatest innovation was his industrial research laboratory in Menlo Park, New Jersey, the first of its kind in the United States. His engineers often worked shoulder to shoulder, rather than in separate offices. Because of this arrangement, they constantly bounced ideas off one another, adding to the environment of creative collaboration and innovation.

Institutional legacy. Edison's initial companies morphed into General Electric, which remains one of the most innovative companies in America.

159

Even 100 years after his death, no organization or individual has taken Thomas Edison's place as a powerhouse of innovation.

What is Innovation?

So, what is innovation? Innovation is doing things differently. It is making creativity useful. But it is so much more. Many people and organizations who sincerely wish to be innovative do not know where to start. They think that "innovation" is some kind of silver bullet that has to come from a creative genius, not mere mortals.

Not so. Ordinary people with ordinary means can innovate.

Innovation is about changing the rules. Giotto, the Italian Renaissance artist, changed the rules for Christian art. He depicted people as three-dimensional beings, rather than the two-dimensional beings other medieval artists thought them to be. Giotto changed the rules, and the Renaissance was born.

Innovation is about questioning assumptions. What are the operant questions in your industry or business? Can you question them, or even reverse them? Oprah Winfrey questioned the assumption that one could not talk about intimate issues on national television. We all know how that turned out.

160

Innovation is about intense customer focus.
How well do you know your customer? How well
do you know every customer's inner needs and
wants? What tasks do your customers need done?
The makers of Kindle know that people will keep
reading, and will always want a more efficient way
to do so. They created a machine that closely
equates to the process of reading, yet is easier to
use than carrying around stacks of books.

Innovation is about creating a "wow" factor. Can
you produce a product or service that far exceeds
the customer's expectations or the standards in the
marketplace? Progressive Insurance can get you a
quote online in ten minutes. Not only that, but they
can quote their competition. Compare that to the
old two-hour session with an agent in your living
room and a three-week wait for your quote.

**Innovation is a radical break from the past and
the tweaking of a product or service.** Innovation
is a longer, harder, better, stronger, clearer pencil.
It is also a new class of writing utensils.

**Innovation is observing accidents and aberra-
tions**. Accidents and aberrations happen, and innovations occur as a result of those abnormalities. Yet
it takes an observant mind to see the accidents and
understand what they mean. The man whose

chocolate bar melted in his pocket might have just been mad, but he used the incident to understand a heating source and invent the microwave.

Innovation is entering another box. When we spend too much time in one box or paradigm, we become captured inside that box. To think differently, we must leave our comfort zones and enter new boxes—whether they are other industries, companies, cultures, or ways of living. Many universities and companies give their employees sabbaticals in order to refresh their thinking. Others use cross- training to help employees understand different parts of the company.

Innovation is crafting a climate for creative collaboration. Innovations come from organizations that are primed for it. World-class companies such as General Electric, Apple, 3M, and Amazon create environments where innovation can happen. These companies produce strings of innovation and tend to the cultural garden that continues to allow the innovative spirit to blossom.

There is no silver bullet for innovation. Innovation is hard work. It is discipline. It is a long and winding road, fraught with potholes, dips, and boulders. But innovation is what creates wealth and excitement and enthusiasm. Enjoy the ride.

Bibliography

Amabile, T. 1998. "How to kill creativity." *Harvard Business Review.* September/October, 1998.

Barker, J. 2005. *Five Regions of the Future.* London: Penguin.

Barker, J. 2009. *Innovation at the Verge.* St. Paul: Star Thrower Distribution.

Barker, J. 2001. *The Business of Paradigms.* St. Paul: Star Thrower Distribution.

Bughin, J., M. Chui, and B. Johnson. 2008. "The Next Step in Open Innovation." *McKinsey Quarterly.* June, 2008.

Carter, S. 1999. *Renaissance Management: The Rebirth of Energy and Innovation in People and Organizations.* London: Kogan Page Limited.

Chowder, K. 2003. "Eureka." *Smithsonian Magazine.* September, 2003; p. 92.

Christensen, C. M. 1997. *The Innovator's Dilemma: When New Technologies Cause Great Firms to Fail.* Boston: Harvard Business School Press.

Collins, J. 2001. *From Good to Great.* New York: HarperBusiness.

Drucker, P. 1985. *Innovation and Entrepreneurship: Practice and Principles.* New York: Harper and Row.

Drucker, P. 1985. "The discipline of innovation." *Best of Harvard Business Review.* 1985.

Fast Company Magazine. April, 2000.

Freidel, R. (1996). "The Accidental Inventor." *Discover Magazine.* October 1996, p. 69.

Gelb, M. 2007. *Innovate Like Edison.* New York: Dutton.

Goleman, D. 1995. *Emotional Intelligence.* New York: Bantam.

Gryskiewicz, S. S. 1999. *Positive Turbulence: Developing Climates for Creativity, Innovation and Renewal.* San Francisco: Jossey-Bass.

Hamel, G. 2006. "The why, what, and how of management innovation." *Harvard Business Review.* February, 2006; p. 72–84.

Hargadon, A., and R. I. Sutton. 2000. "Building an innovation factory." *Harvard Business Review.* May–June, 2000.

Hargadon, A. 2003. *How Breakthroughs Happen: The Surprising Truth About How Companies Innovate.* Boston: Harvard Business School Press.

Heath, C., and D. Heath. 2007. *Made to Stick.* New York: Random House.

Leonard-Barton, D. 1995. *Wellsprings of Knowledge: Building and Sustaining the Sources of Innovation.* Boston: Harvard Business School Press.

Leonard, D., and J. F. Rayport. 1997. "Spark innovation through empathetic design." *Harvard Business Review.* November-December, 1997.

McKinsey and Co. "How companies approach innovation." *McKinsey on Innovation.* 2007.

Michalko, M. 1991. *Thinkertoys.* Berkeley: Ten Speed Press.

Miller, W. C. 1998. *Flash of Brilliance: Inspiring Creativity Where You Work.* Reading, Massachusetts: Perseus Books.

Pink, D. 2005. *A Whole New Mind.* New York: Riverhead Books.

Senge, P. 1990. *The Fifth Discipline.* New York: Currency Doubleday.

Schrage, M. 1989. *No More Teams.* New York: Doubleday.

Skarzynsky, P., and R. Gibson. 2008. *Innovation at the Core.* Boston: Harvard Business School Press.

Stacey, R. D. 1996. *Complexity and Creativity in Organizations.* San Francisco: Berrett-Koehler Publishers, Inc.

Tapscott, D., and A. Williams. 2006. *Wikinomics: How Mass Collaboration Changes Everything.* New York: Penguin.

"Powers of Creation." 1996. *Discover Magazine.* October, 1996.

"Best Innovations of 2007." *Time Magazine;* November 12, 2007.

About the Author

Richard Brynteson's mission is to help engineers become more personable, executives less fearful, and managers more thoughtful. As an organizational consultant, executive coach, and graduate-school educator, he helps corporate and public-sector clients apply innovation techniques to these work processes and products in order to make them efficient and more effective.

He has held marketing, strategic planning, and management positions at two Fortune 500 companies known for successful product development and innovation efforts, where he introduced new products (some producing $1M in annual sales), trained nationwide sales forces for the new products, and developed new overseas markets.

Richard left the corporate sector in 1988 to begin private consulting and do graduate work. He holds a Ph.D. in Education from the University of Minnesota and an MBA in marketing and finance from the University of Chicago, and is currently a professor of management and marketing at Concordia University in St. Paul, Minnesota, where he has taught since 1992.

He continues to lead workshops and seminars in change management, marketing, leadership training, EQ, and business ethics, and continues to provide consulting services to clients here and abroad. He can be contacted at brynteson@csp.edu.

Made in the USA
Lexington, KY
01 October 2014